O Mighty Warrior!

Also by Shelley Wilburn:

The Healing Path, A 30-Day Guide to Walking Healed and Living in Freedom

Walking Healed, A Journey of Forgiveness, Grace, and Hope

Walking Healed Companion Bible Study

Warrior Princess, Ignite Your Inner Warrior

To Eric —

Arise,

O Mighty Warrior!!

Igniting the Warrior Within

Shelley Wilburn

You are chosen of God!

Shelley Wilburn

Walking Healed
M I N I S T R I E S

Mismatched Socks Publishing

O Mighty Warrior! Igniting the warrior within

Copyright © 2022 Shelley Wilburn

First edition

Nonfiction, Inspirational Education

Chapter head images courtesy of Pixababy.com. Thank you.

Images on "What Does a Mighty Warrior Look Like" page property of Southern Illinois Worship Center, Used by Permission

Cover design by Paul Ruane

Print: 978-0-9864311-6-6
E-Book: 978-0-9864311-7-3
Library of Congress control number 2022904185

Scripture quotations are taken from the Holy Bible, New Living Translation (NLT), copyright ©1996. Used by permission of Tyndale House Publishers, Inc. Carol Stream, IL USA. All rights reserved.

Scripture quotations are taken from the Amplified Bible, Old Testament. Copyright © 1965, 1987 by the Zondervan Corporation. Used by permission. All rights reserved. Scripture quotations are taken from the Amplified Bible, New Testament. Copyright © 1954, 1958, 1987 by the Lockman Foundation. Used by permission.

Scripture quotations marked "NKJV" are taken from the New King James version. Copyright © 1982, Used by Thomas Nelson, Inc. Used by permission. All rights reserved.

Scripture taken from THE MESSAGE. Copyright © 1993, 1994, 1995, 1996,2000, 2001, 2002. Used by permission of NavPress Publishing Group.

Scripture taken from The Expanded Bible (EXB). Copyright ©2011 by Thomas Nelson. Used by permission. All rights reserved.

Scripture taken from the New Century Version®. Copyright © 2005 by Thomas Nelson. Used by permission. All rights reserved.

Scripture quotations are from the ESV® Bible (The Holy Bible, English Standard Version®), copyright © 2001 by Crossway, a publishing ministry of Good News Publishers. Used by permission. All rights reserved.

Scripture taken from the NEW AMERICAN STANDARD BIBLE®, Copyright ©1960,1962,1963,1968,1971,1972,1973,1975,1977,1995 by The Lockman Foundation. Used by permission.

The Holy Bible, Berean Study Bible, BSB, Copyright ©2016, 2020 by Bible Hub, Used by Permission. All Rights Reserved Worldwide.

O Mighty Warrior! exposes the enemy for who he is and the tactics that he uses to steal, kill, and destroy us. More importantly for us men, *O Mighty Warrior!* guides us in the discovery of our identity in Christ so that we can be the Mighty Warriors we were designed to be! Men, learn your place in God's big plan for humanity through *O Mighty Warrior!*

~ Tim Williams Ed.D., Senior Executive Pastor,
Southern Illinois Worship Center, Herrin, Illinois

As I read O Mighty Warrior, I am encouraged as well as inspired to remember number one, who God is in my life, but more than that, who I am to God. When you read this book you will be inspired as well to grow into the man of God He wants you to be, and to live out your calling. You are a Mighty Warrior! Claim the victory over your life, in Jesus' mighty name!

~ Scott Kelley, Corrections Officer, Williamson
County Sheriff's Department, Marion, Illinois

When I read O Mighty Warrior I picked up on several references to battle, armor, and staying in the Word at all times. To men, those things catch our attention. As a men's influencers director, staying in the Word is something I always tell the men. Men have trouble with what I call the "in between" time. That's the time between when they leave the parking lot on Sunday until the next Sunday. Men often do not realize they have Spiritual authority. In O Mighty Warrior, it spells it out quite vividly. It's time for men to stop being afraid and to take a stand. Let go of our pride. Be watchful, stand firm in the faith, be strong and act like MEN!

~ Keith Szablewski, Men's Influencers,
Director, Southern Illinois Worship Center, Herrin, Illinois

Dedication

For all the Mighty Warriors in my life:

    Don A. Wilburn, my husband; protector, defender, and knight. The head of the mighty warriors in this family.

    Logan, my son; the warrior who runs head-on at every threat.

    Brett Wininger and Clint Milam, my sons-in-law; the warriors who love and support my daughters and grandchildren.

    Radley, Abraham, Jude, Jensen, Jax, and Chase, my grandsons; you are the squires, the up-and-coming mighty warriors. Watch and learn, dear hearts.

Table of Contents

Note from the Author

Instructions for What to Expect Through This Book

When I first wrote *Warrior Princess; Ignite Your Inner Warrior* for women, I never thought, years later, that I would be reconstructing it to inspire men. Yet here we are!

While writing *Warrior Princess*, I allowed the Holy Spirit to guide me to the passages in which He wanted me to highlight. A remarkable thing began happening that I only noticed as I came closer to getting done with the study. I want to share it here as well because before we get started because I want you to be on the lookout for it. I believe it is important for you to know through this reading; nearly every long passage referred to the LORD in all capital letters. This is monumental. It means something.

Several years ago, while doing a Beth Moore* Bible study, I learned that (according to Beth) in the formal versions of the Bible, as opposed to most modern paraphrases, when you see references to *Lord*, capital "L," this is the Hebrew transliteration, a form of *Adonai*, emphasizing God's lordship and His position as Master. When you see references to *LORD* (in all caps), the Hebrew transliteration is *YHWH* and emphasizes His position as covenant maker and keeper (this one is my favorite). When you see references to *God*, the Hebrew transliteration is *Elohim* and emphasizes His position as universal Creator.

What a rich blessing to learn the meanings of His name in just how it is projected or spelled out in Scripture! I feel so blessed by this revelation. I want you to be blessed as well. Therefore, throughout this study, whenever you see any reference to the Lord, regardless of spelling, I want you to circle it and refer back to this description in order to get a deeper meaning of the passage and what He is saying to you. I'll remind you periodically.

Now here we are, ready to take the journey. Take a few moments and familiarize yourself with this book. Throughout, you will discover hints to your true identity. They are called *links*. They are words that describe things about you which we find in God's Word and they will be in italics and bold so you can reference them later throughout the book. As you discover them, I have provided a page in the back of the book titled, *Who I Am in Christ*. This is where I would like for you to write those links. When you finish this book, you will have a clearer picture of who you truly are because you will have discovered it in God's Word and can then dub yourself His Mighty Warrior.

As you read, let the Holy Spirit speak to you. And as you learn, get bold and write notes in the margin of your book. Use it as a guide, a treasure map if you will, to not only discover your true identity but also the One who calls you by that name.

I'll walk with you through this book and at the end we will have a special chat. Be sure to meet me there.

Glossary of Armor

Crown

A royal or imperial headdress or cap of sovereignty: *diadem*.

Belt

A strip of flexible material worn especially around the waist as an item of clothing or as a means of carrying something. A similar article worn as a corset or for protection or safety or as a symbol of distinction.

Helmet

A covering or enclosing headpiece of ancient or medieval armor.

Breastplate

A piece of metal that covers a person's chest and that was part of the protective clothing (called armor) that soldiers wore in the past.

Shoes (sandals or boots)

An outer covering for the human foot typically having a thick or stiff sole with an attached heel and an upper part of lighter material (as leather).

Shield

A large piece of metal, wood, etc., carried by someone (such as a soldier or police officer) for protection.
Something that defends or protects someone or something.

Sword

A weapon with a long metal blade that has a sharp point and edge.

Chainmail (mail)

A kind of protective clothing (called armor) that is made up of many tiny metal rings that are linked together and that was worn by knights and soldiers in the Middle Ages.
Flexible armor of interlinked metal rings. First use: 1822

Foreword

I am a forgetful person.

Just ask my wife. I have a hard time remembering where I put my glasses. One time I spent half a day searching for the remote control for the living room television, only to find out I had stuck it in the refrigerator. I am a person who needs constant reminding on where stuff is. I will leave notes in my phone, reminding me of where stuff is located in the garage, in the basement, etc. At work I need to remember about three different passcodes; one for the printer, another to get into the building, yet another code for my computer login. Still, there are times where I drive up to the ATM machine and I'll forget my PIN number. It's been like that my entire life! I have to have a reminder. Plain and simple, I need help remembering.

Maybe that's why I truly appreciate what Shelley Wilburn has done with her book, *O Mighty Warrior*. This is a *huge* reminder of who I am in Jesus Christ! As I was reading the pages of her work, I was reminded over and over again about who I am, and to Whom I belong. It's easy to forget. I think Jesus knew we would forget, that's why He instituted the Lord's Supper. When we get going in our hectic hustle-and-bustle life, working a job (or two), trying to be the best husband, father, friend, care-giver, church member, everything to everybody type of guy, we can forget. The world will start to chip away at us.

Then we get tired.

That's when the enemy of our souls likes to creep in and whisper lies into our ears.

I don't know what it is but, those lies will stick in my head like a dart on a dart board. On the other hand, the truth, which I've been told pretty much since birth, gets pushed to the side. I'm just being honest. Make no mistake about it, there is a battle going on between good and evil, and it is time for you and me to shake off the lies the enemy has told us. Maybe you've struggled with those lies your entire life as well, and it's constantly playing in the back of your mind like a broken record. It's time to armor up!

O Mighty Warrior is more than just a book. The pages are filled with God-breathed Scripture and instructions on how you can get rid of the enemy's lies which are buzzing around in your head. They will be replaced with truth. It's refreshing!

To get the most out Shelley's work, I suggest you use this book as a workbook. Take your time and write down those notes as you go. You'll be glad you did.

It's time to wake up! It's time to remember who you are! It's time to take the enemy and land a drop-kick straight to his face!

It's time to rise up, O Mighty Warrior!

Kent Zimmer
99.9 WOOZ-FM Radio (Z-100)
Carterville, Illinois

Introduction

There is a battle going on. It has been going on since before time began. God was fully aware of it, but He chose to move forward with His plan. Why? Because, God's plan is infallible. It's perfect. Yet, while there has been seemingly one disaster after another, each one has worked perfectly into His plan...including the creation of *you*.

Believe it or not, you too are part of God's wonderful, amazing, larger-than-life plan. That is exciting! But let's address some things before we begin to move into the position He has created for each of us.

Many of you don't know your part in this great plan. Even more of you have no idea who you really are. You just don't know who you are *in Christ*. As such, how then can you operate in the gifts and the calling God has on your life?

Maybe you're wondering, *"There's a calling on my life? How can that be? God couldn't possibly use me!"* Oh, Mighty Warrior, there truly *is* a call on your life and God absolutely *can* use you. Through the pages of this book we are going to take a journey to uncover your true identity. By the time we finish, you will be equipped to take your place as God's own Mighty Warrior.

It may sound ridiculous to you right now. Trust me, it's not.

In His Word, God says a lot about us. That is our identity. We *are* who God says we are. He says we are more than conquerors. That means we are victorious in everything and then some. We exceed, or go beyond that victory. Why? Because when Jesus defeated Satan once and for all, He did more than just win the battle over death. Jesus got up from the grave. He beat hell so we wouldn't have to go there, eternally separated from Him. He did all that so we wouldn't have to suffer. He conquered it all, took back the keys to death, hell, the grave, the kingdom, everything—He did it for you. He did it for me.

Maybe you're saying, "Well, I'm saved, isn't that all there is?" Oh, Mighty Warrior, being saved is so much more than a ticket to heaven. There is so much more to it than that, and too many are missing out on their *more* because they stop at salvation. You are more than a victor. You go beyond that into the realm of royalty, to having the power to tell the devil to take a hike.

For an example of how our prayers are prevented from being answered, read Daniel 10:12-14.

You need to know the devil wants to mess you up. He will stop at nothing to make things miserable for you, including hindering your prayers. There are times when there are spiritual wars going on above you to prevent your prayers from being heard. However, you have the power and the authority over the devil and he hates you for it.

There are many who are discovering that daily. They are learning their true identity and stepping into their role as Christ followers, mighty men of God, and because of that, there's an army rising up. They have drawn the lines; battle lines, and stepped over them into battle. It's time to put on your full armor and prepare to run, full-on, at the enemy, sword raised, battle cry on your lips.

You will be victorious, make no mistake. You will not be defeated. There will be no casualties of this war. None. For this war is already won. All that you, me, and all of us have to do is stand, then watch the Lord fight for us. And He *will* fight for us.

Don't misunderstand: if we do nothing, this battle won't be fought. We must rise and stand our ground in order to be victorious.

Our identity is at stake here. Our enemy is trying to steal the very essence of who we are as a people. He's also using many different areas and people to do it. It's up to us to put our foot on his neck and take back what is rightfully ours. It *can* be done. It *must* be done.

Are you ready?

1 Valley of Dry Bones

Bringing the Dead Back to Life

" 'Dry bones, listen to the word of the LORD!' ...Then you will know that I, the LORD, have spoken, and I have done what I said. Yes, the LORD has spoken!' "

~ Ezekiel 37:4b, 14b, NLT

What if I told you that you were more than you know? What if I were to tell you that you were actually royalty—for men, a prince? Would you believe me? Would you laugh, snicker, roll your eyes? What if I told you that not only are you royalty but you're a warrior as well?

You may not feel like a warrior right now, much less a prince. I can totally understand and identify with your feelings.

I have been there myself. Maybe you're thinking or even saying, "How can I be a warrior? I'm always intimidated. I never stand my ground. I always back down, or give in. How can I possibly be a warrior? Yeah, forget about me being a mighty warrior."

I get that.

Oh, dear friend, God has something to say to you. In fact, He has a lot to say to you. With that, we are going to move into discovering your true identity because you have a Prince pursuing you. You have a King Who loves you crazy, madly, deeply. Sounds like a fairytale, doesn't it? Maybe a little unbelievable. It's not. It's for real, He is for real, and your true identity is definitely for real.

You have been living in the Valley of Dry Bones for so long you've been led to believe you're just dried up, useless, worth nothing to God. But it's all a lie and it comes straight from the enemy of your soul. You, oh mighty ones, *are* each a Mighty Warrior.

First, though, we have to really know who we are in Christ. Walk down any street, store aisle, parking lot, home, school, anywhere and you will see dry bones; men and women who merely exist yet not really live. Why is that? Some look happy. Some act happy. Their clothes, shoes, cars, trucks, even their homes all dictate happy, healthy, thriving human beings. True. Physically, they are.

However, look deep inside each one of them and even ask them pointedly if they are happy and they will tell you a completely different story.

I wish I was more successful.

I wish my job was secure.

I wish people understood.

I wish I was in better health.
I wish I looked better.
I just wish people would see me.
No one knows the pain I suffer.
I deal with depression.
I'm so afraid.
I deal with anxiety.
I'm not worth anything.
I'm not smart.
I'm so alone.
I have no one.
No one cares about me.
I just wish I had a real friend.

On, and on, and on these statements could go and would probably describe many people you know, or maybe even yourself. Some may even lie and tell you they are perfectly happy and their lives are perfect. Yet, inside they live in shame and guilt, not wanting anyone to know the truth because it would be devastating to them.

It can happen to anyone, even Christians. This is how the enemy tricks us into believing that we aren't good enough; especially not good enough for God. Believing the lies of the enemy, we wither and withdraw into ourselves, thereby becoming nearly lifeless inside, merely existing. That's how the enemy prevents us from living the abundant life God wants us to have.

We live in a valley of dry bones and don't even know it. But God has other plans for those bones. He wants them to live and breathe again. He wants *you* to live and breathe again. Can dry bones live again? Let's find out.

In the book of Ezekiel, the LORD took Ezekiel the prophet in the Spirit and showed him a valley filled with dry bones. These bones were actual dried up, dead bones; lifeless, without skin. Yet, God had a plan and showed Ezekiel something profound.

Read Ezekiel 37:1-14 below, from the New Living Translation.

The LORD took hold of me, and I was carried away by the Spirit of the LORD to a valley filled with bones. He led me all around among the bones that covered the valley floor. They were scattered everywhere across the ground and were completely dried out. Then he asked me, "Son of man, can these bones become living people again?"

"O Sovereign LORD," I replied, "you alone know the answer to that."

Then he said to me, "Speak a prophetic message to these bones and say, 'Dry bones, listen to the word of the LORD! This is what the Sovereign LORD says: Look! I am going to put breath into you and make you live again! I will put flesh and muscles on you and cover you with skin. I will put breath into you, and you will come to life. Then you will know that I am the LORD.'"

So I spoke this message, just as he told me. Suddenly as I spoke, there was a rattling noise all across the valley. The bones of each body came together and attached themselves as complete skeletons. Then as I watched, muscles and flesh formed over the bones. Then skin formed to cover their bodies, but they still had no breath in them.

Then he said to me, "Speak a prophetic message to the winds, son of man. Speak a prophetic message and say, 'This is what the Sovereign LORD says: Come, O breath, from the four winds! Breathe into these dead bodies so they may live again.'"

So I spoke to message as he commanded me, and breath came into their bodies. They all came to life and stood up on their feet – a great army.

Then he said to me, "Son of man, these bones represent the people of Israel. They are saying, 'We have become old, dry bones – all hope is gone. Our nation is finished.' Therefore, prophesy to them and say, 'This is what the Sovereign LORD says: O my people, I will open your graves of exile and cause you to rise again. Then I will bring you back to the land of Israel. When this happens, O my people, you will know that I am the LORD. I will put my Spirit in you, and you will live again and return home to your own land. Then you will know that I, the LORD, have spoken, and I have done what I said. Yes, the LORD has spoken!"

It may seem unrealistic to think, or even believe, that dry, dead bones can come back to life. Yet, here we are reading that yes, in fact, they did. The LORD often gives us visions, dreams, and even real-life experiences in order to teach us that He is true to His Word. He also does it to teach us that we are His, and fully equipped to carry out His instructions, His tasks. However, many times, He has to take us through a series of tests in order to prove it to us.

In the passage above, after showing Ezekiel the valley filled with dried-out bones, the first thing the LORD asked Ezekiel was whether or not those bones could become living people again. Ezekiel's answer was, "*O Sovereign LORD, you alone know the answer to that.*"

Do you think that Ezekiel didn't know, or wasn't completely sure of the answer? That would be me (although God knows all things, including our thoughts). However, Ezekiel could have answered the way he did so he didn't make himself seem prideful. Give the glory back to the LORD, because we cannot make the dry bones live again. But the LORD? That's another story altogether.

Instead, the LORD gives Ezekiel a task: speak a prophetic message to the bones that He, the LORD, is going to put breath into them and make them live again, that He is going to put flesh and muscles on them and cover them with skin, as well as put breath into them and they would come to life.

For what reason did He do this? So they would know that He is the LORD!

In the New Testament, just after Jesus rose from the dead, He appeared to His Disciples. They had been hiding in a locked room, afraid of the Jewish leaders. However, Jesus was suddenly before them, proving He had risen just as He had promised.

After showing them His wounds, they were all filled with joy. Then Jesus encouraged them by saying, *"Peace be with you. As the Father has sent Me, so I am sending you,"* (John 20:21, NLT).

In the next verse, Jesus did something amazing. Read below:

Then he breathed on them and said, "Receive the Holy Spirit."

Jesus breathed on the Disciples and they received the Holy Spirit. They became truly alive. In the book of Ezekiel, the LORD told Ezekiel to speak a prophetic message to the bones and say to them that the Sovereign LORD said He was going to put *breath* into them and make them live again.

If you read that again, you will read where the bones began to rattle and actually stood. They were put back together and they did live again. But let's read and see what else God said about the bones.

Then he said to me, "Son of man, these bones represent the people of Israel. They are saying, 'We have become old, dry bones – all hope is gone. Our nation is finished.'"

~Ezekiel 37:11, NLT

Although the dry bones are a metaphor and represent the people of Israel, they could very well represent us today. In the following verses, I find it exciting what the LORD says He will do.

"I will put my Spirit in you, and you will live again and return home to your own land. Then you will know that I, the LORD, have spoken, and I have done what I said. Yes, the LORD has spoken!" ~Ezekiel 37:14, NLT

God has great plans for each of us. He wants to breathe life back into us through His Spirit, the Holy Spirit, so we can live again (spiritually) and return Home someday. Our heavenly home.

The enemy tries to wear us down and make us believe we are no longer useful to God or anyone. Through the circumstances of our lives, we shrivel and waste away until we resemble those dry bones in the valley. Or, like the Disciples, we lock ourselves away in fear.

However, Jesus debunks every attack of the enemy. Read below.

*"The thief comes only in order to steal and kill and destroy.
I came that they may have and enjoy life, and have it in
abundance (to the full, till it overflows)"*

~John 10:10, Amplified Bible

The enemy (the devil) comes to try to mess up our very
lives. I'm sure you can think of many areas of your life in which
you feel he's trying to steal, kill, and destroy things, even in
your own family; your peace, faith, joy, marriage, job, ministry,
etc. We often feel as if we are being tempted and attacked in
every direction. Jesus knows what we're going through,
because He lived it all too. He understands and He cares.

In Hebrews 4:14-15, New Living Translation, we have this
encouragement:

*So then, since we have a great High Priest who has entered
heaven, Jesus the Son of God, let us hold firmly to what we
believe. This High Priest of ours understands our weaknesses,
for he faced all of the same testings we do, yet he did not sin.*

Jesus has faced everything we have faced, or ever will
face, yet with one difference: *He did not sin.* He did this so He
could know what we're going through and be able to help us
walk through those times as well.

Have you noticed in Ezekiel, the spelling of the LORD's
name? Remember, the Hebrew transliteration is YHWH
(pronounced Yahweh) and emphasizes His position as *covenant
maker and keeper*. If you look back through that passage, you
will see that He was in fact making a covenant with Ezekiel. He
even said in verse fourteen, *"Then you will know that I, the
LORD, have spoken, and* I have done what I said. *Yes, the
LORD has spoken!"* (emphasis is mine).

Now, maybe you're wondering what this has to do with us today, in this time. My answer is, *everything*. In Hebrews 4:12-13, New Living Translation, it states:

"For the word of God is alive and powerful. It is sharper than the sharpest two-edged sword, cutting between soul and spirit, between joint and marrow. It exposes our innermost thoughts and desires. Nothing in all creation is hidden from God. Everything is naked and exposed before his eyes, and he is the one to whom we are accountable."

When you open God's Word, your Bible, do you feel as if Someone just stepped into the room? I do. Why? Because Someone just did. That's the presence of the Lord. His Word is definitely, and without a doubt, alive and powerful. I find that exciting!

God's Word also cuts to the deepest recesses in our bodies, *cutting between soul and spirit, between joint and marrow.* God sees everything about us, yet still loves us deeply. Though we wear clothes, we are exposed naked before Him (Hebrews 4:13). Does that make you feel vulnerable? Me too.

Additionally, though we are exposed before God, He sees everything we do and we are accountable for everything we have ever said, thought (even the hateful things we have thought), done, or experienced, God *still* wants to do a great work in us and with us. Remember, Jesus experienced the same challenges. He understands our hurt, anger, sorrow, sickness, depression, abuse, everything. There is nothing you can name right now that Jesus does not understand. You are not alone. You are not left out.

You may be wondering what all this has to do with discovering your true identity. It has everything to do with it, because you have to know the why and the what-for of the things you're experiencing in order to push back the veil of your identity. Let's keep moving forward.

Psalm 33:13-15, New Living Translation, says this:

The LORD looks down from heaven and sees the whole human race. From his throne he observes all who live on earth. He made their hearts, so he understands everything they do.

God has great plans for each of us.

If God made us (and He did), He definitely understands everything about us, what we do, and our motivations. He knows us from the inside out. Therefore, why is it so hard for us to understand or even believe that He has a great and wonderful plan for us?

Simply put, there is a thief who wants to steal, kill, and destroy everything about us (John 10:10). Yet, in Psalm 32 it says that God is our hiding place; He protects us from trouble, and He surrounds us with songs of victory (v.7). In verse eight it states that the LORD says He will guide us along the *best* pathway for our lives and will advise us and watch over us.

By surrounding us with songs of victory, wouldn't that tell you that He brings deliverance? I think so. That's a link to discovering your identity. You are **delivered**. So even though our enemy, the devil, comes to steal, kill, and destroy, God surrounds us with songs of victory guiding us to the best pathway.

There is never a moment when God isn't leading, guiding, advising and watching over you. Therefore, another link in discovering your identity is realizing you are smart and can in fact, learn. In other words, you are *teachable*.

Debriefing:

So far in this journey we have learned that in order to discover our true identity we must be brought back from the dead (spiritually speaking). We need to have life breathed back into us. We need to be rescued from the Valley of Dry Bones, to rise up from the ashes. We also need the Holy Spirit. We can no longer afford to lie in the dust or hide in fear. There is no place for either.

Arise, O Mighty Warrior! We are only beginning.

Be sure to turn to your **Who I Am in Christ** *page and write the links you found.*

Further Reading:
Ezekiel 37:1-20
Psalm 32

2 Battle Lines

Every soldier must know, before he goes into battle, how the little battle he is to fight fits into the larger picture, and how the success of his fighting will influence the battle as a whole. ~Bernard Law Montgomery

Even before time began battle lines were drawn. It started in heaven when Lucifer decided he could be as great as or greater than God. Of course, God stepped over those lines and *like lightning* Lucifer fell. Now, where most people get confused is when they refer to Lucifer, aka Satan, as coming from hell. He's not there. When Lucifer fell, he fell to earth. I

> To read about the fall of Lucifer refer to Isaiah 14:12-15, NKJV.

would imagine he fell with a mighty big *thud*. And that is where we will find our battle lines today.

God knew the larger picture before He ever created time. He knew, yet He chose to proceed with Creation, time, even you and me. We ask why, yet we cannot see the bigger picture. Only God can see it. It must be a pretty awesome picture in order for Him to continue to allow us to wake up every morning and do the things we do. The enemy still threatens, attacks, and tries to destroy God's plans. Let's look at one of his most famous attacks.

In Genesis, chapter three, is where we find one of the enemy's most famous attacks:

NOW THE serpent was more subtle and crafty than any living creature of the field which the Lord God had made. And he [Satan] said to the woman, "Can it really be that God has said, You shall not eat from every tree of the garden?"

~Genesis 3:1, Amplified

Described as subtle and crafty and disguised as a snake, Satan does not spark fear into Eve. Many believe it's because she was used to all the animals, bugs and so forth, and there was no sin, so there was no reason for fear. Instead, the enemy spawned confusion by questioning the very words of God, *"Can it really be that God has said...?"* If the devil can make anyone question God's Word, he brings confusion into your life which can cause you to say and do things contrary to, or opposite of what God's perfect plan for you truly is. Hence, Eve eating of the forbidden fruit and Adam doing likewise.

When we disobey God's instructions, we begin to venture away from Him eventually finding ourselves out of His will. Once we do, the enemy then begins to whisper into our minds those negative, derogatory comments and soon we begin to question God's love for us. But he doesn't use his own words. He will use our own.

I've done too many bad things.
God is mad at me.
I can't serve in church anymore.
I'm too old.
I have to get my life straightened out first.

What a blatant lie.

These are the daily battle lines we need to be aware of. Hear me out, I said *daily*. Yet if we know our enemy and his tactics, we can come against him swiftly, precisely, and victoriously.

Let's take a look at some true statements from God's Word to see if we can gain some counter measures.

For God is not the author of confusion but of peace, as in all the churches of the saints. ~1 Corinthians 14:33, NKJV

If you feel confused, it isn't God who is causing it. Peace is what you should have. Lack of peace should be a warning that the enemy may be attacking you. Confusion is another warning. God doesn't want us to be confused about Him or anything in His plans for us. He wants us to be at peace.

Don't stop there. Let's move on and see what other strategies we can uncover.

For God has not given us a spirit of fear, but of power and of love and of a sound mind. ~2 Timothy 1:7, NKJV

I find this passage particularly profound and powerful. In verses three through six of Second Timothy, the Apostle Paul is writing to his charge, Timothy, to give him encouragement. He is bringing to light Timothy's heritage and his faith, reminding him how his grandmother and his mother had raised him in trusting the Lord. Paul also reminds Timothy to stir up the gift of God within him through the laying on of his (Paul's) hands.

This gave me encouragement that even the saints of old dealt with the attacks of the enemy in much the same way in which we do today. Paul reminds Timothy of what God has given us; power, love, and a sound mind. That should be enough to encourage and spur *you* on.

In addition, we find three more links to your identity, Mighty Warriors. You are **powerful**, you have **love**, and you have a **sound mind**. We can even go as far as to add a fourth link and say you are **fearless**. Even though at times you do feel fear, we all do; in many places in the Bible, it says we should not be afraid.

God does not want us to be afraid, although it's a normal feeling. However, we also should not operate according to our feelings. Instead, we should acknowledge our fear, then move forward. Whatever we are preparing to do, we should do it even if we are afraid. When we do, we may find that our fears are unfounded and just another tactic of the enemy to prevent us from doing what God has called us to do.

Fear, feelings of powerlessness, confusion. These are areas where the enemy likes to poke. I say that because very often it feels as if we are being poked in sensitive areas. Now you have some positive weapons with which to counterattack the enemy when you feel that barb.

A big key to dealing with fear is to realize we won't ever

be completely rid of it. Fear will often just show up unexpectedly. We must recognize it and deal with it right away. In other words, take care of it. Be confident we have what it takes to deal with it, be active and never give up.

Let's look at a couple more counter measures before we move on.

In the fourth chapter of the book of James, he talks about drawing close to God. One of the biggest countermeasures we can take against the devil is to stay as close to God as we possibly can. We are told to be subject (submit) to God. When we subject ourselves (or submit) to God, we are merely making ourselves humble before Him. We respect Him. We love Him. That is *key* in coming against the devil. We must resist the devil, and God's Word says he will flee from us. The Amplified Bible says to "stand firm against him" (James 4:7). When we come close to God, then He will come close to us.

Oftentimes we find ourselves having been disloyal to God. Regardless how that happens, and many times it happens due to our attitude, arrogance, and/or pride, when we realize our mistake (humbling ourselves), we can reconnect with Him quickly.

James 4:10 from the New Living Translation says it like this: *"Humble yourselves before the Lord, and he will lift you up in honor."*

> God wants to lift us up, to elevate us.

God wants to lift us up, to elevate us. That can mean more than just raising our spirits and making us feel better. God has such great big plans for us! The enemy wants to thwart those plans by constantly searching for our weak spots so he can attack us. He will poke, prod, pinch, and provoke in any and every possible area of our lives to cause us to stumble, get confused, distracted, angry, or ill.

How, then, can we stay on top of things and ahead of the enemy? Ephesians 6:17 from the New Living Translation says we should put on salvation as our helmet and take the Sword of the Spirit, which is the Word of God.

Salvation is our *helmet*. Armor is necessary at all times. Spiritual armor. We will cover wearing armor in another chapter, but how do we protect ourselves? The second part of that verse says we are to also take the Sword of the Spirit, which is the Word of God.

God's Word, our Bible, is a sword. A mighty sword. Remember, we talked earlier about the Word of God being alive and powerful? It's not only powerful but sharp *(Refer back to Hebrews 4:12-13 in the last chapter)*. God's Word is very important not only in defeating our enemy, but in discovering our true identity.

By staying in the Word we stay one step ahead of the devil at all times. How encouraging!

You may be wondering "how can I stay in the Word *all* the time?" I understand. We all have things to do. It's life. But in the moments when we are between tasks, we can grab a couple of verses from the Word. In our quiet moments before we wake the kids (or the kids wake us!), we can grab the Bible and read. Or listen to worship music in the car.

Post some of your favorite verses throughout your house, car, truck, and various other places so that wherever you go, God's Word is there. Talk to Him periodically throughout the day. Talk to Him as you lay your head down at night before you go to sleep.

The enemy has drawn the battle lines and he will entice you to cross over them many times. What if you were prepared beforehand and *crossed the line* ahead of him? Refer back to James 4:7. Strategic planning is necessary and God is the best at strategy.

Every small battle we fight fits into God's bigger plan. We don't know the big plan, but He does. So, as we cross the battle lines daily, we must be prepared. Let's take a look at how.

Realize You Have Authority

As a child of God, a Christ follower, a Christian, God has gifted you with spiritual authority. But don't let that go to your head. You must keep your wits about you, dear warrior. Yet you cannot afford to be timid.

> God has gifted you with spiritual authority.

With authority comes responsibility. Maybe you don't want that responsibility. Or maybe you aren't ready. Regardless of whether we want that privilege or are ready for it, we still have it and it's up to us to use it in a way that brings glory to God.

So, what do we do with this authority? What do we use it for? Oh, dear friends, this will be amazing to discover. When we talked about stepping over the battle lines, we are stepping directly into battle. Though our battles may not necessarily be what we think they are. We are entering a very real but different realm.

It says in 2 Corinthians 10:3 (NKJV), *For though we walk in the flesh, we do not war according to the flesh.*

We are human. We are going to have physical arguments, fights, and wars. However, those are because of *spiritual warfare*. We must realize that our war is in the supernatural; therefore, we must prepare spiritually.

In every war, weapons are used. According to verses 4-6 of 2 Corinthians, the weapons of our warfare are not carnal but mighty in God. They are used (or to be used) for three things: pulling down strongholds, casting down arguments, and every high thing that exalts itself against the knowledge of God.

Remember, many of our battles are in the mind. Therefore, we use our spiritual weapons to bring every thought into captivity and into the obedience of Christ (see v. 5).

When we take every thought captive, or bring our thoughts under control, we step over the battle lines of thoughts, emotions, and mental turmoil. In doing so, we are being obedient to the call God has on our lives. We can also help others become obedient with their thoughts and actions (v. 6). This is where our authority comes to use.

In every battle, the enemy plots against you while you strategize on how to defeat him. Our enemy never stops. He never blinks (remember he's like a snake and snakes have no eyelids). He creeps and prowls around, watching. We can never stop, either. We cannot put too much thought into our enemy because he uses the same tactics that he's used since the beginning. Therefore, we shouldn't have to think too hard in order to defeat him. We just need to pay attention and make sure our focus is on the Lord.

One of my favorite passages in the Bible is from 1 Peter 5:8-9. Below, I have included it from the Amplified Bible, because I think it resonates with extra verbiage in not only exposing the enemy, but in warning us both how to be on guard against him and encouraging us that we are not alone.

Be well balanced (temperate, sober of mind), be vigilant and cautious at all times; for that enemy of yours, the devil, roams around like a lion roaring [in fierce hunger], seeking someone to seize upon and devour.

Withstand him; be firm in faith [against his onset – rooted, established, strong, immovable, and determined], knowing that the same (identical) sufferings are appointed to your brotherhood (the whole body of Christians) throughout the world.

In this passage, the first thing we are told is to be cautious... *all the time.* For God to warn us to be on the alert at all times, don't you think it was for a reason?

With the devil continually stalking us, we are a target. There are the battle lines again. Why would we let our guard down for even one moment? We must protect ourselves at all times for impending attack.

We are told to withstand the enemy. In the above passage, we are instructed to do it by being firm in the faith, our faith, to be rooted, established, strong, immovable, and determined. Those are some mighty strong instructions. However, sometimes we can feel as if we are the only ones going through this battle. Don't worry. God even provides encouragement by telling us that we aren't alone in being stalked by the enemy. *All* of our brothers and sisters in Christ deal with the same things we do. Every one. Though while we are going through those tough times, it often seems a lonely place to be.

In 1 Peter 5:7 from the New Living Translation, it says we are to *"give all our worries and cares to God..."* All of our worries and cares. Every bit of them. Don't leave even one tiny thing out. Why? Because He cares for us.

If you look at the definition of the word *all*, you will discover something profound. I learned this a few years ago and was amazed, although why should I be amazed by what the LORD does. At any rate, in the original Greek and Hebrew, the word for all is simply this: *all*. So, when it says in Scripture to give all our worries and cares to God, it means all of them.

In the New King James Version, it says to cast; to throw. Throw all your worries and cares to God. "Cast all your cares upon Him for He cares for you."

Therefore, although we go through many trials, things that cause us worry, anxiety, fear, etc., we are to cast, or throw, everything upon the LORD. Give it all, every bit to Him. He cares about us because He created us.

We do this because we are a target for the enemy. He will use every means he can, including using other people as a distraction to cause trouble for us. But there is always something we can do. Cry out to God.

In review, 2 Corinthians 10:3 reminds us that we are human and we don't wage war as humans do. We do it in the spiritual; in prayer. Therefore, when we cry out to God, He promises that He will be there for us.

Remember, Jesus defeated our enemy, the devil, over two thousand years ago. Because of what Jesus did on the cross, Satan has no power, although many give him power by allowing him to whisper lies over them, thereby they believe they are defeated. It's time to take a stand. It's time to begin asserting our spiritual authority.

Let me reiterate, our battle is not in the natural. It's in the spiritual. Therefore, we must be prepared spiritually for the battles we will face. Though sometimes people may be the ones who seem to be attacking us, remember, the enemy is behind the lines. He's in the background. But what do we do about the ones who say they too, belong to Christ?

The Apostle Paul addressed this subject in his letter to the Roman Church, as he explained his own spiritual authority. Take heart, dear warrior, his spiritual authority is also ours. Look at what he says below:

Look at the obvious facts. Those who say they belong to Christ must recognize that we belong to Christ as much as they do. I may seem to be boasting too much about the authority given to us by the Lord. But our authority builds you up; it doesn't tear you down. So I will not be ashamed of using my authority. ~2 Corinthians 10:7-8, NLT

According to the Apostle Paul, our spiritual authority comes from Christ. It builds us up, it never tears us down. We would do well to remember that. But to cement that thought for you, let me give you a quote from Jesus out of Luke 10:18-20 from the New King James Version:

And He [Jesus] *said to them, "I saw Satan fall like lightning from heaven.*

"Behold, I give you the authority *to trample on serpents and scorpions, and over all the power of the enemy, and nothing shall by any means hurt you.*

"Nevertheless do not rejoice in this, that the spirits are subject to you, but rather rejoice because your names are written in heaven" (emphasis is mine).

Did you get that? Jesus gave us authority, spiritual authority, to trample on (step on, tread, walk on, etc.) serpents and scorpions. This isn't the literal critters, although they won't hurt you either. This is demons, evil spirits, and minions of the devil. But Jesus also gave us authority over all the power of the enemy. Did you catch that most important word? *All.* Not just a little bit of it. Not just certain aspects of it. *All of it!*

Oh, Mighty Warriors, do you not get the magnitude of your authority? How exciting! But there's more. Read on.

Jesus also said that nothing shall by any means hurt you. Nothing. However, there is a stipulation to this. It's not a catch-22 situation, just merely a gentle warning, or reminder. Basically, don't let this go to your head.

Even though the spirits are subject to us, because of our authority, Jesus reminds us that we are to rejoice, be happy about, the fact that our names are written in the Book of Life! We are registered in Heaven!

Knowing that we belong to Christ and our names are written in the Book of Life should be the most important thing to us. It should give us the most peace and happiness. Christ loves us; therefore, He would never allow anything to hurt us. That's why He gave us authority over all things, including the power of Satan, our enemy, which renders him powerless. Once we realize this, we can move forward in our journey of discovering our true identity and walking in the freedom Christ died for us to have.

Our spiritual authority not only comes from the Lord, it is meant to build each other up, not tear one another down. This is yet another link to our identity; we have *spiritual authority*. Although we will encounter others who may seem to want to silence us, or maybe who don't understand the authority we claim, we cannot and should not be ashamed of the authority the Lord has given to us. Instead, we should walk in our authority with boldness. This has great bearing on our identity and should also give us insight into the ploy of our enemy.

You must know the enemy is afraid of you. But he's not afraid of who you *were*. He doesn't care about your past, although he uses that against you whenever he can, to keep you tied up emotionally, mentally, spiritually and, yes, even physically. If he can keep you living in the past, you'll never move forward into your future, the one God has laid out for you.

No, dear Warriors, Satan is not afraid of who you *were*. He's afraid of *who you might become*. As a child of the Most High God, you were a threat upon conception. So, the enemy began plotting against you, drawing those *battle lines*. If he can keep you behind the battle lines, he thinks he can prevent you from rising up into who God intended you to be. Once you realize who you are in Christ, you become an even bigger threat to the enemy.

Therefore, we must learn to practice our authority and not allow ourselves to be dominated by our enemy, Satan. We must be trained in spiritual warfare. However, if we are always oppressed and dominated in the physical life, it will not feel normal to us to war in the spiritual. We will not possess the natural skill to war spiritually. This is why we must learn to use and exercise our spiritual weapons.

By understanding these battle lines, we can now move forward into discovering our role as a Mighty Warrior and how to walk in that identity with confidence. We can also operate in a position of victory and help rescue and lead other warriors.

Debriefing:

In this part of our journey, we have studied how battle lines have been drawn since before time. Though we are human, we do not fight in the physical but in the spiritual. We know that Satan draws the lines every day. He stalks us, always looking for ways to attack. He also moves the lines, which is cheating. We also learned God has declared us victorious! Even though we come under spiritual attack, our God-given authority can pull down strongholds, and should build up, not tear down. We should use it to help rescue and lead others to discover their identity in Christ.

Don't give up yet, O Mighty Warriors. Our story only gets more exciting!

Now turn to **Who I Am in Christ** *and write the links you found in this section.*

Further Reading:
Isaiah 14:12-15
James 4:7
2 Corinthians 10:3-6

3 Basic Training

We are not transformed by rising to the occasion. We rise to the occasion because we have been transformed. How are we transformed? By the renewing of our mind. By convincing our heart that God is good, even when our circumstances are not.

~ Donna Partow, *This Isn't the Life I Signed Up For* (2003)

When you accepted Jesus as Lord and Savior, you were immediately given an appointment, or assignment, into the army of the Lord. Your *Basic Training* began—or rather, was to begin. You were given all the equipment necessary to carry out your mission.

However, not everyone understands the training. They may see the Words on the page, but have a hard time understanding them or even believing them. We are *all* called. Though our assignments may differ greatly, yet they are still similar. How then, do we prepare for our assignment? We must re-train our brains. We must renew our minds. We must have Basic Training.

As in any branch of the military, the enlisted must be trained in the most basic of operations. They must learn discipline. They must learn the rules of the branch of the military they are in. They must learn how to listen to and respond to their commanding officer, and most importantly, how to strategize, fight, and win against the enemy. They also must learn how to operate in their specialized field.

The enlisted must re-train their brain to think and act like the soldier they are. No longer are they like civilians, but someone entirely different. Why would it be any different for warriors in God's army? As a child of the King, we do have privileges, as we studied in the last chapter. However, we still need to be trained, always on the ready, always alert and always prepared. We cannot take our training lightly. It's important in discovering our identity.

In basic training, the enlisted begin with the basics. So will we.

Our brains need re-training. I'm not talking about learning the rules of whatever denomination you are in. I'm talking about learning to hear and obey the LORD. That comes from reading His Word (the Bible). Our brains need to be given a refreshing and pure alternative to the everyday push of the world. Therefore, renewing our minds

Renewing our minds daily is essential in training.

daily is essential in training.

In Romans 12:2 we are given explicit instructions for that very thing. I'm including it, from the Amplified Bible, because I believe it gives a little more depth to the meaning of being renewed and why.

And do not be conformed to this world [any longer with its superficial values and customs], but be transformed and progressively changed [as you mature spiritually] by the renewing of your mind [focusing on godly values and ethical attitudes], so that you may prove [for yourselves] what the will of God is, that which is good and acceptable and perfect [in His plan and purpose for you]. ~Romans 12:2, Amplified Bible

To conform means to change to whatever, or whomever, is making the rules. Maybe that sounds familiar to you today. But instead of conforming to the standards of the world, the society in which we live, we are told to renew our minds, to focus on godly values and ethical attitudes. In other words, focus on what God says to do.

In doing that, we are then transformed (changed) by the renewing of our minds into God's will for us. And God's will is always good, acceptable, and perfect. God always wants what's good for us.

Also keep in mind, we have an enemy constantly stalking us, looking to destroy everything about us. That alone should keep us focused on godly values and ethical attitudes. We need continual renewing of our minds in order to stay prepared and ready to defeat him. That means renewing every day.

A key strategy is to memorize Scripture. In doing so, we always have the Word with us and in us. That is powerful stuff.

How do we keep the Word within us? According to Psalm 119:11, we hide God's Word in our hearts, which keeps us from sinning against Him. However, we are not perfect. We *will* mess up. We don't always do it on purpose, but it happens. When we do make a mistake, the enemy will use that to bring an attack against us. Yet the Holy Spirit helps us in bringing the Word to mind so we can open our mouth and speak the Word, defeating the enemy once more and putting him in his rightful place, under our feet.

God laid out the strategy for defeating the enemy long ago. Jesus showed us how to use it.

Our training is preparedness for when the devil will whisper lies into our minds and for when we encounter temptations that bring us to the point of decision. Though the devil cannot hear our thoughts, he doesn't have to know them. All he's concerned with is getting you to believe *his* lies. Remember, the battlefield is often our minds.

Even Jesus dealt with enemy attack. How He handled it was to speak God's Word, *out loud*, directly to the devil. God laid out the strategy for defeating the enemy long ago. Jesus showed us how to use it. It's up to us to follow through. By using His example, we can do likewise.

The enemy uses the same three tactics today as he did when he tempted Jesus. He will use our physical needs, emotional needs, and our pride or desire for significance or power to cause us to slip. If he can succeed, he will then begin the attacks in our minds, trying to convince us that God no longer loves us, needs us, or wants us. If we believe the lies, we slip further into the pit of self-pity, self-loathing, and isolation. This is why training is so very important, along with staying close to our brothers and sisters in Christ.

Oftentimes, God will allow us to be tempted in order to test our loyalty to Him. Don't misunderstand, God does not cause bad things to happen to us. Though He does *allow* it in order to either make a point with you or with someone around you.

Your faithfulness in such situations is crucial. For example, in the military when the troops go into various combat scenarios, they are training for the possibility of enemy attack. How they handle it teaches and prepares them, and determines their ability. It helps them to grow as a soldier. They get stronger both physically, mentally, and emotionally. Our training as warriors is very similar; only add "spiritual" to that list.

How, then, does this help us discover who we are in Christ? Knowing that even Jesus Himself was tempted by the devil gives us assurance that we are not alone. There is nothing we will face that Jesus hasn't faced. Because of His encounters and His suffering, He can comfort us, give us understanding, love, and support in everything we face.

He is the Source of all comfort. He comforts us in all our troubles. He does this so, in turn, we can comfort others whenever they are troubled. The same comfort we received from God we are now able to give to another in need. That's basic training. Learn from the trials we go through so that we can help others go through what we once did. In 2 Corinthians 1:3-7, New Living Translation, we are told:

All praise to God, the Father of our Lord Jesus Christ. God is our merciful Father and the source of all comfort. He comforts us in all our troubles so that we can comfort others. When they are troubled, we will be able to give them the same comfort God has given us. For the more we suffer for Christ, the more God will shower us with his comfort through Christ.

Even when we are weighed down with troubles, it is for your comfort and salvation! For when we ourselves are comforted, we will certainly comfort you. Then you can patiently endure the same things we suffer. We are confident that as you share in our sufferings, you will also share in the comfort God gives us.

When we go through troubles, God's Word says it's for our comfort and salvation. Though it may not make sense at the time, in our future encounters it will make perfect sense.

In the passage above we find another link to our identity. Though it may not seem like a piece of who we are, it's good to know we are **comforted** by God in all the things we go through. We don't go through anything alone. Not only does everyone go through trials and suffering, Jesus did as well.

Because of what He went through, He became our High Priest; Someone who knows and understands everything about us—our weaknesses, trials, and even our sufferings. There is nothing He doesn't know about or understand because He, Himself, went through those very same things with one exception; He did not sin (see Hebrews 4:14-15).

It is for this very reason that we are told in verse sixteen, *"So let us come boldly to the throne of our gracious God. There we will receive his mercy, and we will find grace to help us when we need it most"* (NLT).

When we need it most, we will find grace to help us when we come boldly before God and receive His mercy. He is there for us. *Always*. He is our Commander in Chief; therefore, we should always follow His directions because they are always given in love and for our benefit.

Friends, you and I are important to God. We have been since before time. If we look back in Genesis, God even said, *"It is not good for the man to be alone. I will make a helper who is just right for him"* (Genesis 2:18, NLT). This isn't a sexist or racist remark. It's truth. God created woman to be the helper to man, to come alongside him and be one with her husband. Man and woman are a team. When they both have a relationship with Jesus, together they are a powerful force to be reckoned with. They are a dual threat to the enemy.

However, since the beginning, the devil has been trying to drive a wedge between man and woman, husband and wife. He started in the Garden of Eden and who did he zero in on? The woman. This is why it is very important for women, as well, to discover their true identity and train for the battles ahead. We can no longer allow ourselves to be deceived by our enemy.

> We can no longer allow ourselves to be deceived by our enemy.

Men and women have been oppressed for centuries. Controlled, sold into various forms of slavery; physical, sexual, even mental and emotional. There are many children, young girls and boys, and women sold into sex trafficking every day. There are also many who are being rescued daily because those who have found their freedom are rising up and going into battle to free these precious souls.

Even as you read this, God is freeing people all over the world, not just from human trafficking, but from depression, drug abuse, prostitution, gambling, pornography addiction, physical abuse and much more. He is elevating men and women to new and exciting heights. When God frees you of something that has kept you in bondage or slavery, it's exhilarating. Once free, it is important to re-train and renew your mind in order to use your story to help free someone else who suffers in the bondage you were once held captive.

Whatever it is that controlled you, God wants you to use your story to help another. He has chosen you to bring that good news to unshackle the chains holding someone else down. You could be the key that Jesus uses to unlock their chains.

Maybe you don't think you're qualified. Maybe you aren't sure you have what it takes. You may wonder if God even knows who you are. There were also people in the Bible who felt that way, unsure they were qualified or unsure that God knew them, much less called them to do something specific for Him.

But look at what the Lord said to the prophet Jeremiah, from Jeremiah 1:5, from the Amplified Bible.

"Before I formed you in the womb I knew you [and approved of you as My chosen instrument], And before you were born I consecrated you [to Myself as My own];
I have appointed you as a prophet to the nations."

Although this was said to Jeremiah, it also applies to us today. As well, in Ephesians 1:4 from the New Living Translation it states, *"Even before he made the world, God loved us and chose us in Christ to be holy and without fault in his eyes."*

In these passages, God says He knew us before He made the world and before He even formed us in our mothers' wombs. More than that, He even approved us, chose us, consecrated us, and appointed us. In addition, He loved us and chose us to be holy and blameless in His eyes!

We may have a hard time accepting this truth. However, God not only knew us before He created us, He *chose* us. That's not all. The things we just read above are more links to our identity; *approved, chosen, consecrated (set apart), appointed, loved, holy, without fault (blameless)*.

Though the enemy blasts accusations our way, God's Word says something very different. Because God loved us, we were chosen long before the devil started accusing us. How can we be accused if we are blameless? This is why training is so important.

In basic training in the military, the enlisted have a schedule. They rise early, are required to meet together, they exercise together, learn together, work together, live together, eat together, and expected to get along. *Together*. The troops also learn the tactics of the enemy, how to identify him, how he speaks, acts, thinks, and even how to defeat him. The same training applies to us as God's sons.

God set up our training long ago. Every saint before us had a purpose and an appointment to teach, preach, and write letters so that we would learn, grow and be able to carry on God's message to future believers. God isn't dumb. Because He is omnipresent, He knew the end before the beginning. Therefore, He made a way for every generation, even you and me.

We learn from reading our Bibles. We train by listening to our pastors, mentors, and teachers. There are many throughout our lives who have gone before us who will help lead, teach, and train us in our journey. Our job is to listen with open ears, mind, and heart, then ask the Lord to give us wisdom to discern the direction He wants us to take.

We will also encounter many who claim to be teachers, preachers, and prophets who are not. They will tell us things which are not completely true. If we are not properly trained, we will run the risk of being deceived and led down a destructive path. That's a dangerous place to be. But how do we know that what is being said to us is true?

My dear friends, don't believe everything you hear. Carefully weigh and examine what people tell you. Not everyone who talks about God comes from God. There are a lot of lying preachers loose in the world.

Here's how you test for the genuine Spirit of God. Everyone who confesses openly his faith in Jesus Christ – the Son of God, who came as an actual flesh-and-blood person – comes from God and belongs to God. And everyone who refuses to confess faith in Jesus has nothing in common with God. This is the spirit of antichrist that you heard was coming. Well, here it is, sooner than we thought!

My dear children, you come from God and belong to God. You have already won a big victory over those false teachers, for the Spirit in you is far stronger than anything in the world. These people belong to the Christ-denying world. They talk the world's language and the world eats it up. But we come from God and belong to God. Anyone who knows God understands us and listens. The person who has nothing to do with God will,

*of course, not listen to us. This is another test for telling the
Spirit of Truth from the spirit of deception.*

~1 John 4:1-6, The Message

To me, the above passage is very profound because I can
see this unfolding in our world today. There are many who are
standing before the masses, leading thousands into various
things. The people are following along, blindly, believing that
their leader is giving them the truth, causing them to rise up and
stand for a cause when in reality they are being led into eventual
destruction. This is not a political statement, nor is it race-
related. It's *spirit*-related. Plain and simple. As Christ-
followers, how then do we get past this? It takes us back to basic
training.

I reiterate, the first thing we are told to do is to not believe
everything we hear, but we are to carefully weigh and examine
what we are told. To test for the genuine Spirit of God, the
simplicity of it is to listen to how others speak. If they profess
Jesus Christ openly, that He is the Son of God, in the flesh, then
they have come from God and belong to Him. If they don't, then
they are liars. Don't believe a word they say.

That, my dear Warriors, should tell you more than you
need to know. Not only do we *come* from God, we also ***belong
to God***. Therefore, anyone who tells you they know God should
speak with and show love, not hate.

In the verse above, we also find another link to our identity.
However, let's confirm it in another passage from God's Word.

Acts 17:28-29 from the New Living Translation tells us,
*"For in him we live and move and exist. As some of your own
poets have said, 'We are his offspring.'*

"And since this is true, we shouldn't think of God as an

idol designed by craftsmen from gold or silver or stone."

There is the next link to your identity. You are God's *offspring*. His *child*. That is so exciting to me. Let's say this statement out loud.

I am the child of the Most High God!

The Word says this is true. Therefore, since you are one of God's children, His offspring, how does that make you feel? Who is He to you? Write your thoughts below.

_____

_____

_____

_____

_____

_____

_____

Debriefing:
We have come a long way in this chapter in discovering our true identity. It is not only important to renew our minds daily, but to also have good teachers and mentors in our lives who can help us in our basic training. We've learned where we come from and to Whom we belong. We've also studied how to discern the Spirit of Truth from the spirit of deception. Knowing these things gives us a good foundation so we can move further in our journey.

It's getting more exciting. Let's move forward.

Turn to **Who I Am in Christ** *and write the links you found in this section.*

Further Reading
Psalm 119:11
Matthew 4:1-11

4 Your Assignment

"Whatever God shows you to do – obey it quickly."
~Rich Mendola, "Joy in the Holy Spirit…in the Desert"
The Complete Guide to Christian Quotations, pg. 320

By now, you have a growing list of adjectives in the back of this book, describing who you are as God's precious one. Not only are you all those things, but so much more.

In this chapter, our journey takes us even deeper into discovering more about who God says we are. Along with what we've already uncovered we will add more and more to our list.

Being a warrior, one of God's chosen, His offspring, we discover that we all have an assignment. Some say it's our calling. Others call it our mission. Nevertheless, whatever we name it, assignment, calling, mission, hopes and dreams, desires, it's still an assignment and it comes from God. What we do with it depends on our obedience to Him as our Heavenly Father.

Each of us has been given a place in God's agenda. That should tell you how important you are to Him. Each one of us is part of God's wonderful, amazing, larger-than-life plan. We all have a call on our lives. We have all been given special talents and abilities and are expected to use them to help and encourage others in this life journey.

Regardless of our individual talents and abilities, our assignment is that we are all called to restore the people of God into a right relationship with Him. We are called to encourage, inspire, build up, heal, nurture, teach, and yes, even to warn our brothers and sisters in Christ. By warn, that doesn't mean to tear down, insult, ridicule, or mock. A loving word from a brother or sister in Christ, a fellow Warrior, is what those who are in bondage need.

Let's dive right into discovering what our assignment is and how we are to carry it out. In the process, look for more links into your identity.

Going back to the book of Ezekiel, look at what God tells the prophet in Ezekiel 33:7-9 from the New Living Translation.

"Now, son of man, I am making you a watchman for Israel. Therefore, listen to what I say and warn them for me." ~Ezekiel 33:7 (NLT)

"Now, son of man, I am making you a watchman for the people of Israel. Therefore, listen to what I say and warn them for me.

"If I announce that some wicked people are

sure to die and you fail to tell them to change their ways, then they will die in their sins, and I will hold you responsible for their deaths.

"But if you warn them to repent and they don't repent, they will die in their sins, but you will have saved yourself."

Those are some pretty strong words. Though they were spoken many years ago, they are still just as powerful and relevant and even apply to us today. There is also a link into our identity. It is found in verse seven. We, as warriors, have been appointed as **watchmen** for our brothers and sisters in Christ. A big responsibility, yes. However, it does not negate who we are, nor does it mean we can use our authority for personal gain.

Ezekiel was appointed watchman for the people of Israel. His assignment was to warn the people if he saw them falling into sin. If he did not warn them, and they died in their sins, God would hold Ezekiel personally responsible. However, if Ezekiel did warn the people, but they did not listen to him and they died in their sins, God held them personally responsible.

God also never promises that when we bring a message to our brothers and sisters, they will listen. However, if we fail to do what God has given us to do and one of them falls into peril, then we *are* responsible.

Before we delve deeper into that, let's look a little more into our assignment to get a better understanding of what God has called us to do.

In Jeremiah 1:5-12 (I use New Living Translation), God told the prophet Jeremiah to go where He told him to go and to say what He told him to say. He also instructed Jeremiah to not be afraid of the people because He, God, would be with him and protect him. Such profound instructions. However, then He reached out and put His words into Jeremiah's mouth, giving him a most noble assignment; to stand against nations and kingdoms, to uproot and tear down, to destroy and overthrow some, and to build up others.

After appointing him, God showed Jeremiah a branch from an almond tree. He then told him that meant that He, God, was watching and would certainly carry out all of His plans. That should encourage us today as well.

God is always watching. He will also always carry out all of His plans. Regardless of whether we are obedient, God's plans never fail and His message will be delivered one way or another. It would be prudent for us as His children, to carry out the message He gives us regardless of the repercussions we may *think* we'll incur from those around us.

Personally, I would rather give a difficult message to a brother or sister in Christ and risk *their* retaliation than to keep my mouth shut and be held responsible for their actions because I didn't deliver a message from our heavenly Father.

Please note: God is not mad at you, nor is He waiting for you to mess up so He can zap you into oblivion. Oh, Mighty Warriors, our God is a loving Father and even if we do mess up and neglect to speak when the Holy Spirit prompts us to speak, God still loves us and will use us for His glory if we will come humbly to His throne of grace and repent of our mistakes because He's just that good. He's just that awesome.

But what if you do miss an opportunity? What if you miss an assignment? What then? Does God remove your calling?

Look at what Romans 11:29 from the New Living Translation says below.

For God's gifts and his call can never be withdrawn.

If we miss an opportunity, if we blatantly disregard an assignment from the Lord, it doesn't mean that we lose our gifts. They are still there. God doesn't make mistakes. God doesn't make us obey. He doesn't bow to us or to what we want. He is perfect. He is sovereign. He knows exactly what He's doing. Our decision to disregard His instruction is not a surprise to Him. Our choice to obey or disobey is strictly up to us. That's the beauty of free will. We can choose what we want to do. Our decision will also either grant us a blessing or cause us to miss a blessing.

> For God's gifts and his call can never be withdrawn.
> ~Romans 11:29

Isaiah 55:11 from the New King James Version, states:

"So shall My word be that goes forth from My mouth; It shall not return to Me void, But it shall accomplish what I please, And it shall prosper in the thing for which I sent it."

When God puts forth His Word, it accomplishes what He pleases and it prospers. So, whether we choose to be obedient or not, God will get the job done. Now, how does that connect to our identity in Christ? Very simply put, our obedience determines how successful we are in accomplishing God's Word. If we are who God says we are, wouldn't it be in our best interest to do what He has called us to do? Let's move on.

As a watchman, we have a great responsibility. Yet sometimes those we are assigned to speak to just won't listen. Sometimes the most difficult people to reach are the ones we are closest to.

Then Jesus told them, "A prophet is honored everywhere except in his own hometown and among his relatives and his own family." ~Mark 6:4, NLT

Our own family may reject us because of our belief or our testimony. I have experienced this myself. For years I suffered severe depression, anxiety, and even verbal abuse from many sources. However, one day I determined that I was done living in this way. I sought out healing from a God whom I wasn't sure would hear me. But He knew my heart and graciously placed wonderful, godly people in my path to help me (watchmen). Through His divine intervention, I was healed and no longer do I dwell in that ugly place.

My healing, while a miracle, is not accepted by everyone I meet or talk to. But that's okay. While it's a sad situation, I must press forward and do what God has called me to do. This is what you must do as well, dear sojourners, dear warriors.

Though we don't carry out God's message for our honor, we also must realize that not everyone will hear our message, including family. We will then be presented with a decision: stay quiet and stay in the good graces of family or friends who will not acknowledge our position? Or, follow a sovereign God, who loves us more than the world?

Let's take a look at a sister who was placed in a high position and then presented with a life-and-death situation, not only for her family, but for herself. How she responds will mean life or death for all involved. Yet, she becomes deeply distressed about what to do.

I'm talking about Esther. And while this book is geared for you, dear brothers, mighty warriors, Esther has something we all would be smart to take note.

Although queen, Esther had a calling from God: save her people from destruction. It distressed her greatly. However, her cousin, Mordecai, gives her some wise advice. It has become a statement we've all adopted when giving advice to others, even today.

"If you keep quiet at a time like this, deliverance and relief for the Jews will arise from some other place, but you and your relatives will die. Who knows if perhaps you were made queen for just such a time as this?" ~Esther 4:14, NLT

For such a time as this. Esther was placed in the palace with the king and found favor with him in such a way that he would do anything for her. Though she had a great enemy and was even afraid and distressed because of the threat hanging over the lives of she and her people, she was encouraged to take a stand and speak up. Her obedience saved a nation.

We could learn a great lesson from Esther today. We are living in the time God has chosen for us. We also have been given a great calling for such a time as this. We will also come up against opposition. Remember from our previous chapters that we have a great enemy who will use every tactic to try to defeat us and keep us from the call God has on our lives. He will also do everything he can to prevent us from discovering our true identity.

So, what happens if we choose *not* to follow through with our call? There will also be times when we just blatantly go the opposite way when God gives us an assignment. What then? What happens when we do that? Know that God never gives up on us. He gives us every opportunity to do what's right. He will even go to the depths of the sea to get our attention.

If you read in the book of Jonah, the word of the LORD came to Jonah not once but twice! Once, before he disobeyed and the second time after Jonah had spent three days and nights in the belly of the great fish.

God never changed His mind. His words to Jonah were the same. *"Arise, go to Nineveh, that great city…"* In chapter one it states to *"proclaim against it."* In chapter three, God says to *"preach and cry out to it."* However, in chapter three, God said for Jonah to tell them what He, God told him to say (from chapter one). Therefore, God's Word did not change.

When God gives you an assignment and you disobey, He will give you another chance to redeem yourself and be obedient to His call. However, if you still disobey, He may re-route that call to someone else to do. You are not condemned, O Mighty one—you just missed a blessing.

In the book of Judges, Deborah was judging Israel at that time. Deborah was a prophetess and would sit under a palm tree where the people of Israel would come to her for judgment (Read Judges 4:4-24).

God chose Deborah to be in leadership position (the watchman) over Israel during this time period. While Israel was in captivity, God gave instructions for them to get out of captivity. Deborah sent for Barak, giving him explicit instructions that the LORD commanded him to take ten thousand men and He (God) would deploy Sisera, the commander of Jabin's army, and deliver him into his hand. Remember, the LORD had sold the children of Israel into the hand of Jabin the king of Canaan because of the evil they did in His sight. Sisera was the commander of Jabin's army.

Deborah relayed the instructions of the LORD to Barak, even telling him that he would be successful. However, Barak's response was, *"If you will go with me, then I will go; but if you will not go with me, I will not go!"* (Judges 4:8b, NKJV).

When Barak blatantly disobeyed, her response was, *"I will surely go with you; nevertheless there will be no glory for you in the journey you are taking, for the LORD will sell Sisera into the hand of a woman"* (Judges 4:9, NKJV).

Though Barak, along with Deborah, went out against Jabin's army, the army of Sisera fell, but Sisera escaped, hiding in the tent of a woman named Jael (pronounced *Yale*)... who offered him a place to hide and rest. She waited until he had fallen asleep and then killed him by taking a hammer and driving a tent peg into his temple. Hence, just as Deborah prophesied, *"for the LORD will sell Sisera into the hand of a woman"* (v. 9), he was in fact killed by a woman.

Deborah and Jael are two examples of what can be done when we, as mighty warriors, stand and do what God has assigned us to do. This is not about being better than either a man or woman, or a woman doing a man's job, don't get me wrong. However, if we, meaning you or I, man or woman, are called to do a job—it is then not a man's job. It's *our job*, whoever we are. We all have our own special place and position in God's perfect plan. We are not in competition with each other, dear friends. We are all working toward a common goal. We are placed in our time for a specific purpose and plan, ordained by God even before we were conceived.

The point of the story of Deborah, Barak, Sisera, and Jael is that when God gives you or me an assignment and we disobey or decline, He will see His plans through. He will find another who is willing to do what we would not. History is very important for learning how we can better not only ourselves, but our circumstances. Just because there has been depression, cancer, heart disease, addiction, abuse, or whatever your family has in its lineage, it does not mean that it has to continue with you, or even your children, or even their children. Breaking generational curses, for example, is a very important part of our existence. We have that power and we should be utilizing every aspect of our assignment throughout our life walk.

Knowing what transpired before us will teach us and encourage us in our journey. It will help us in discovering who we are in Christ and our place is in God's plan. May we learn from those who have gone before us, through their trials and celebrations, through their victories and defeats.

Though we will have trials and opposition, we must remain confident that God knows what He's doing and therefore trust Him to give us the boldness and confidence to move forward. God is for us. We have nothing to fear.

The LORD says, "I will rescue those who love me. I will protect those who trust in my name." ~Psalm 91:14, NLT

In this passage, the LORD promises to rescue those who love Him. And if we trust Him, He promises to protect us.

There are two links to our identity, dear warriors. We are **rescued** and **protected** by God if we love and trust Him. Read below.

For every child of God defeats this evil world, and we achieve this victory through our faith.

And who can win this battle against the world? Only those who believe that Jesus is the Son of God.

~1 John 5:4-5, NLT

There is another link to our identity in Christ. We are *victorious*. If we love and trust God, we have nothing to worry or fear because He promises that we defeat the evil world. And we do it through our faith. Our faith makes us victorious. In a recent Bible study, I read where faith is translated "fully believing." Do we fully believe? In Him? If we do, it also states that the only ones who can win the battle against the world are those who believe that Jesus is the Son of God!

Despite all the things the enemy throws at us, despite the people who would try to keep us in bondage, in the chains of our past, we can overcome that and be victorious just by having faith in Jesus and being obedient to the call God has on our lives.

Your story matters, dear warrior. No matter what you've been through or are going through now, you matter. You have a story to tell. You have a purpose and God has a plan. You cannot fail unless you refuse to stand. You are promised victory and so much more.

Look at Romans 8:37 below, from the New Living Translation.

No, despite all these things, overwhelming victory is ours through Christ, who loved us.

Now look how the New King James words it:

Yet in all these things we are more than conquerors through Him who loved us.

Overwhelming victory. The New King James says "more than a conqueror." With statements like that, how can we not step out into our calling?

There is another link to your identity; you are a *conqueror*, an *overcomer*.

Through Christ, who loved us, still loves us, will always love us, we can have the confidence and assurance that we will succeed in whatever it is God has called us to do. We just need to step out in faith and obedience.

We talked earlier about being God's children, His offspring, but that isn't all.

And since we are his children, we are his heirs. In fact, together with Christ we are heirs to God's glory. But if we are to share his glory, we must also share his suffering.
~Romans 8:17, NLT

Not only are we God's children, we are His heirs.

Because of Jesus, we share His inheritance. In that passage we find another link to our identity. We are an *heir*. In addition to our shared inheritance with Jesus, our Brother, in order to share in His glory, we must also share the suffering.

We discussed this above. Not everyone will listen to or accept what we have to say. Some will not believe in Him, nor will they believe in our healing, our story, or the blessings He has bestowed upon us. Some, in their own grief or struggles, will not be able to understand a God who loves them unconditionally because they have been blindsided by the enemy.

It all ties together and it ultimately points us directly back to Jesus. We just have to be willing to look, listen, and obey.

After knowing all the things our assignment can bring us, opposition, resistance, battle, etc., how can we defend ourselves? We must be prepared at all times. We will look at that in the next chapter. Get ready, O Mighty Warriors... it's time to suit up!

Debriefing:

In this chapter, we have studied how each of us has a call on our lives. We discovered we have been appointed watchmen over our siblings, called to give them inspiration and encouragement, but also warnings to help them come back to the Lord. We have also learned that our gifts and callings are irrevocable and that even when we miss our call, we can repent and be back in a right relationship with God. Not only that, but we have also discovered not everyone will be receptive to who we are in Christ yet we still have an assignment and God gives us a choice.

Be sure to write all the links to your identity on the **Who I Am in Christ page.**

Further Reading:
Esther 8-9
Jeremiah 1:5-12
Judges 4:4-24

5 Prepare for Battle

This is not suggested; it is commanded. The Bible would not have told us to take up the whole armor of God in order to withstand evil if evil could have been withstood without doing that. ~ Stormie Omartian, topfamousquotes.com

In every branch of the military the troops have a uniform. In fact, they have more than one. They have the everyday uniform they wear when doing their everyday tasks. They have the combat uniforms. And they have their dress uniforms when performing formal duties or attending formal events.

Each piece of the uniform has a specific purpose and meaning. The uniform is not complete unless every piece is worn from head to toe. To leave out a piece of the uniform, the soldier would be considered out of uniform and therefore unprotected.

As mighty warriors, we too have a uniform we wear. We call it armor. We are to wear it at all times, day and night. Our armor is a custom fit, yet one size fits all. Our physical size does not matter. God has armor specially designed to fit you. The best thing about our armor is it's stylish and never goes out of fashion nor is it ever outdated. It goes with everything.

Up to this point we have discussed many aspects of our identity as a mighty warrior, God's chosen, appointed ones. We know that through many circumstances we can become dry bones, hardly alive, yet Jesus wants to breathe life back into us. He wants us to receive the Holy Spirit, who will help us not only in our journey but in discovering who we are in Christ.

We also know that before time began the battle lines were drawn and war was waged upon God's creation: us. We have identified our great enemy, the devil, aka Satan and know that he hates us because he hates God. Therefore, he wants nothing more than to steal, kill and destroy us and everything about us.

However, we also know that we can be prepared for the enemy's attacks. By renewing our minds, changing how we look at the world around us and by remembering that our fight is not in the natural but the spiritual, we have a head start in overcoming the attacks of the enemy.

Perhaps one of the most important things we can do to be prepared is to make sure we have on the *whole* armor

> One of the most important things we can do to be prepared is to make sure we have on the whole armor of God.

of God. *All of it.* We must constantly be covered from head to toe if we are to protect ourselves from the onslaught of the enemy. It wouldn't do for the troops to go into battle without their battle gear on, their protective covering, so why should we as Mighty Warriors be any different?

Let's begin by looking at why we wear the armor in the first place.

A final word: Be strong in the Lord and in his mighty power.

Put on all of God's armor so that you will be able to stand firm against all strategies of the devil.

~Ephesians 6:10-11, NLT

How much of the armor are we to put on? *All* of it. We are not to leave out one piece. Why would a soldier go into battle without being fully protected or fully prepared? He wouldn't. To do so would not only be ridiculous but his very life would be in jeopardy. When we wear all of God's armor, we are strong in the Lord's mighty power. We put on all of the armor so that we will be able to stand firm against all the enemy's strategies.

If we have on armor, then we are preparing for battle. But what kind of battle are we preparing for? Who or what are we fighting against?

"For we are not fighting against flesh-and-blood enemies, but against evil rulers and authorities of the unseen world, against mighty powers in this dark world, and against evil spirits in the heavenly places." ~Ephesians 6:12, NLT

In the previous chapters, we studied that the enemy is constantly on the lookout for someone to attack. The exact words are "someone to devour." With an enemy like that, it would behoove us to be on the ready. We cannot afford to let our guard down.

No soldier goes into battle unprepared. To do so would be life-threatening or even fatal. Why then, would we not wear our spiritual armor at all times? As God's Mighty Warriors, we must be ready, always prepared whether we are in the lull or on the throes of all-out spiritual attack.

> No soldier goes into battle unprepared.

Therefore, put on every piece of God's armor so you will be able to resist the enemy in the time of evil. Then after the battle you will still be standing firm. ~Ephesians 6:13, NLT

In all the things we've learned up until now, one thing we have been assured of is that we will be victorious, more than a conqueror, still standing firm.

We cannot go into battle with our great enemy without knowing how he operates, or how we can and should respond to him. We must also protect ourselves from enemy attack if we are going to still be standing when the battle is over. This is why armor is so very important.

As God's Mighty Warriors, though we are more than conquerors, we must still be ready for attack every second of every day. It cannot be stressed enough. Sure, we let our guard down at times. Yet it is at those times when the enemy takes advantage of our situation to slither in and place doubt, confusion, fear, and even enmity between us and those we love. He doesn't come in from the front lines where we can see him. He will slide in between the cracks in our armor and whisper his lies. This is why we must always be prepared for battle, especially in our minds. Every piece of armor that a soldier, or Mighty Warrior, wears has a purpose. No piece is any less effective than the other. They all serve their purpose in protecting every part of the wearer, and all work together to ensure the best protection when worn together.

Begin to put on your armor by reading the list from Ephesians 6:14-17 below, from the New Living Translation (emphasis is mine).

"Stand your ground, putting on the belt of truth *and the* body armor of God's righteousness.

For shoes, *put on the* peace *that comes from the Good News so that you will be fully prepared.*

In addition to all of these, hold up the shield of faith *to stop the fiery arrows of the devil.*

Put on salvation *as your* helmet, *and take the* sword of the Spirit, *which is the* word of God."

In the very first part of this passage, before putting on our armor, we are instructed to stand our ground. As we stand our ground we are to begin putting on our armor. On the lines below, list each piece of armor and its use.

Piece of Armor	*Use*
_____	_____
_____	_____
_____	_____
_____	_____
_____	_____
_____	_____
_____	_____

Remember, Satan fights with lies. Sometimes the lies of the enemy will sound like truth because it may make sense in our minds, but that's where this slimy snake attacks us. We must make sure we know God's truth. We should wear it like a belt around our waist, protecting us.

Any time we are presented with information we must always compare it to God's Word. Does it line up with what the Word says? If it doesn't, it's a lie. Only believers have God's truth and only God's truth can defeat Satan's lies.

But how do we know the difference between God and the devil? Maybe you feel this way at times. You aren't sure if what you're thinking or feeling is God or the enemy, and you're just a little bit confused. Therefore, how can we truly know?

Our answer comes from 1 Corinthians 14:33 (ESV) which says, *"For God is not a God of confusion but of peace, As in all the churches of the saints..."*

If you're feeling confused, the Word of God distinctly says that God is not a God of confusion. God is the author of peace. If you don't have peace, then my dear brother, you are being attacked by the devil, who loves to twist God's Word into something vile and malicious. He loves to lie to you.

In the book of John, Jesus is teaching in the temple and the Pharisees begin questioning Him, trying to trap Him into saying something wrong so they can condemn Him. But Jesus already knows their hearts and their motives and He calls them out on their lies and where they're getting their lies.

...Then they said to Him, "We were not born of fornication; we have one Father – God."

Jesus said to them, "If God were your Father, you would love Me, for I proceeded forth and came from God; nor have I come of Myself, but He sent Me.

"Why do you not understand My speech? Because you are not able to listen to My word.

"You are of your father the devil, and the desires of your father you want to do. He was a murderer from the beginning, and does not stand in the truth, because there is no truth in him. When he speaks a lie, he speaks from his own resources, for he is a liar and the father of it." ~John 8:41b-44, NKJV

Jesus clearly and boldly tells these Pharisees their father is the devil and that they all want to do what he does. Ouch! He goes further to call the devil out on who he really is, calling the devil a liar.

The devil is nothing more than a murderer and a liar. He is the father of lies. He never tells the truth. Therefore, when we say we should put on the belt of truth and the body armor of God's righteousness, God's Word is our truth. When we saturate ourselves with Scripture (verses from the Bible) we are covering ourselves with His protection against the lies of the enemy. Let's finish putting on our armor.

Wearing God's righteousness as your breastplate protects

your heart because that's where we keep our emotions, self-worth and trust and that's where the enemy often attacks. We are assured of God's approval of us within our hearts. He approves of us because He loves us. We know this because He sent His Son, Jesus, to die for us.

The next part of our armor is shoes. These shoes are, as a friend of mine puts it, "da bomb-diggity." They are shoes of peace. Don't you know, wearing shoes that are ready to spread the Good News of Jesus to those who need encouragement, salvation, healing, or even rescuing when we travel around spreading this Good News, we are bringing peace.

The enemy wants us to think it's worthless and hopeless to try to reach people for Christ. He wants us to think the size of our task is too big and the negative responses will be too much to handle. I know, dear warriors; I experience it every day, as well. Many are the times I've had that imaginary conversation with someone, anyone, who would probably not listen to what I had to say, or invariably argue with me. But that never transpires.

Our shoes of peace which God gives us are the motivation to continue to spread the true peace that only comes from God. Everyone needs to hear it.

Having a shield of faith is extremely important while we are suiting up. Our faith guards us and protects us from enemy attack. Satan likes to throw accusations, insults, setbacks, temptations, and much more at us like fiery darts (or arrows). Our faith acts as that shield, deflecting the fiery darts the enemy fires at us. They may hit, but those fiery darts, fiery arrows, will hit our faith and literally bounce off, proving us unaffected by his attacks.

Speaking again from experience, in 2012 when God healed

me and the Holy Spirit came into my life, I began feeling something that felt like little *tinks* hitting my chest. Yet I couldn't physically feel anything. At first, I wasn't sure. Was I imagining it? But I began to get a mental picture of arrows hitting a shield and breastplate of armor. Metal. It was just a small vision, yet it was there. Was that my imagination? No.

A few nights later, it happened again and I remember telling my husband, "I just figured out what that is. It's my faith! It's so strong right now and the enemy is attacking me, but I don't feel those arrows!"

That's exactly what was happening. I had made the enemy quite angry with my healing and acceptance of the Holy Spirit. But my excitement in the Lord was so strong and my faith had been elevated to new heights in Him that the enemy couldn't touch me at that moment. But the beauty of it all was that God was allowing me to feel in the spiritual so I would know how to react in the physical. What an awesome experience!

While we know that wearing the breastplate of righteousness protects our hearts against the enemy's attacks on our hearts, we also must wear the helmet of salvation to protect our minds. Many men today are being attacked with depression, anxiety, fear, and things they dwell on by thinking daily, worrying about the *what ifs* in their lives. O, Mighty Warriors, this is the oldest trick of the devil!

The enemy will whisper such lies into our minds that once the fear begins, it snowballs into an avalanche that can paralyze us into immobility, preventing us from moving forward into our calling. That's exactly what the devil was going for.

The helmet is a very important piece of armor. It protects the head from injury. In ancient times, the helmet covered more than just the head. It wrapped around the face, protecting the cheeks, eyes, and nose. It was also elongated and covered the neck on the sides and back which prevented an attack from behind or from the sides. Many opponents carried swords, wielding them at will, trying to strike the most tender area, the neck. If an opponent could strike the neck, it would be fatal for the soldier.

A physical helmet protects the head, face, ears, and neck. The helmet of salvation, a spiritual piece of armor, protects our minds from the lies of the enemy. It should remind us of our security in Christ. When the enemy comes, whispering words to bring fear, confusion, and doubt, we can combat with the security that our salvation lends more than just a ticket into heaven. Those beautiful minds of ours are protected, keeping us reminded of exactly who and Whose we are.

We aren't done with armor yet. You may have noticed there is an extra line in the listing of the armor. That's because there is still one piece of armor left, which people often miss when reading about putting on the whole armor. Read on, dear warriors, for the most important piece of protection going into battle.

Look at Ephesians 6:18 below from the New Living Translation, then go back to the list of armor on the previous pages and fill in the blank.

Pray in the Spirit at all times and on every occasion. Stay alert and be persistent in your prayers for all believers everywhere.

Prayer. So very important. Prayer is us seeking a Holy God for our protection, deliverance, salvation, and success. Prayer shows the Lord that we trust Him. Like talking to your best friend every day, your relationship grows ever closer. It's the same way with the Lord. Praying, talking to Him every day, will make your relationship with Him even stronger.

Praying in the Spirit engages the Holy Spirit to give us direction, come to our aid, give us protection, and guide our every step in battling the enemy. Remember, the enemy is already defeated. However, he never gives up. Therefore, we must always be persistent in our prayers. They keep us in relationship with God and also remind our enemy, the devil, that he has no power.

In verse eighteen of Ephesians six, the apostle Paul says we are to be alert and persistent in our prayers, to pray in the Spirit at all times and on every occasion. But we are also to pray for all believers everywhere. All of them.

> No soldier goes into battle without being alert.

No soldier goes into battle without staying alert. Letting down one's guard can prove destructive or even fatal. In the spiritual, we cannot afford to sit idly by, not paying attention. We must stay alert. By staying alert, we keep ourselves always at the ready.

Matthew 7:7-8 (below from the New Living Translation) gives the best explanation of when and for how long we should pray. It comes directly from Jesus.

"Keep on asking, and you will receive what you ask for. Keep on seeking, and you will find. Keep on knocking, and the door will be opened to you.

"For everyone who asks, receives. Everyone who seeks,

finds. And to everyone who knocks, the door will be opened."

Jesus says if we keep asking, seeking, and knocking, we will receive. Not just one or two people, but everyone who asks, receives. Everyone who seeks, finds. And everyone who knocks, the door will be opened. Everyone! No one is left out if they will only be persistent.

I'm so glad we can talk to God all the time and tell Him everything on our minds and hearts, aren't you?

We have come so far already, but we aren't done yet. Now that we are suited up with our armor on, prayed up, standing our ground, we are ready for battle. Keeping that ever fashionable armor on at all times keeps us on the ready. It also lets the enemy know that we know who we are and Whose we are.

Notice we haven't yet had any links to our identity in this chapter. We are laying ground for more to come. We have already written many links to who God says we are. You should have a pretty good idea beginning to float around in your heads. Now wrap it up in your armor and keep it protected.

Though we have studied the importance of wearing our armor continually, it may begin to concern some of you about the actual battle you must face. Every battle is different. Although we are called to the battle frontline, we don't have to fear. We won't battle alone. We are never alone dear, warriors. Though the enemy tries to send fear, confusion, and distraction our way, if we'll keep our wits about us, God will show us amazing and wonderful things.

Throughout the Bible, God has strategically placed prior events to encourage us and embolden us to step onto the battle ground just as our ancestors before us. Once we have all our armor on and are prayed up, all we have to do is stand. Did you hear me? I said, *stand*. Stand and watch the Lord fight for you.

He has promised that.

When Moses led the children of Israel out of Egypt and they came to the Red Sea, they felt hopeless. They had this great body of water before them and the army of Pharaoh quickly gaining on them. But God parted the sea so they could cross on dry land. However, though they crossed, Pharaoh's army followed. I imagine I would have been as terrified as they were, yet God took care of things, just like He promised. Read below.

But Moses answered, "Don't be afraid! Stand still and you will see the LORD save you today. You will never see these Egyptians again after today.

You only need to remain calm [or still]; the LORD will fight for you." ~Exodus 14:13-14, Expanded Bible

Moses mentions one of the most important things we can do when facing battle first in verse thirteen. Do you see it? DON'T BE AFRAID!

Fear is one of the first things that seems to happen when faced with adversity, isn't it? But God tells us throughout the Bible, "Don't be afraid," even in the most terrifying circumstances. He would not have put it in there if He didn't mean it.

Looking back at the previous verses, the next thing Moses told the people to do was to "stand still and you will see the LORD save you today."

When God says to stand still, He's getting ready to do something amazing. It was no different during this time. Moses told the people to stand still and watch. Watch as the LORD saves you.

Say what?

The LORD is going to save me? Yes! I can literally answer that with a resounding *YES!* because I, too, am one of the saved ones. And there is another link to your identity; you are **saved**. You are rescued. Oh, dear warriors, if you could but see and realize how precious you are to Him. Though you are a mighty warrior, you are also a child of the Most High God. He loves you. He cherishes you. He adores you.

So why do bad things happen?

Therein lies the million-dollar question. Because we live in a fallen world, because there is evil in our world, there are so many today who are living below their means. I'm not talking about poverty, although that's also one of the issues. I'm talking about oppression, depression, anxiety, human trafficking, drug abuse, sexual abuse, physical abuse, addictions, and so many other things that are preventing our precious brothers and sisters, God's precious sons and daughters, from living the full, abundant life He created for them.

You may be wondering how that affects you. Maybe you think it doesn't affect you. But it does. Remember, in the previous chapter we discussed that we are Watchmen. We are called to go out and set the captives free. We are to warn our brothers and sisters. We are to help them. Therefore, we will ultimately do battle, not only for ourselves but for those who cannot battle for themselves. However, in that battle, I repeat: we do not fight alone. We must remember that and be encouraged. That should give all of us a little boost of confidence to press forward.

Debriefing:

In this chapter we have discussed wearing the full armor of God and what function every piece of armor serves. We have also learned the enemy never stops in his attacks upon us and that we need to constantly be prepared for battle. However, we can rest assured that we won't have to battle alone because God will fight for us and save (rescue) us.

Be sure to write the link to your identity on your **Who I Am in Christ** *page.*

Further Reading:
Ephesians 6:10-20

6 Worship is Warfare

"You must remember when waging war with the forces of hell, endurance is the name of the game!"
~Rick Renner, *Living in the Combat Zone* (1989)
The Complete Guide to Christian Quotations,
Perseverance #13, pg. 340

[Note: This chapter contains two parts.]

Part One: Stand

War. It's a topic known to all. We don't like it. We don't like to talk about it. Yet there have been wars since the beginning of time. Throughout history the people of God have been in one battle after another. Some they have won. Some they have lost.

If we were to look back through the Bible at the times God told His people to go to war against their enemies, we would see what caused success or failure.

It's no different today. We battle spiritually every day, every minute of every day. That may be difficult to believe, yet it's true. We battle, but with one difference: we win. The tables have been turned. The deck is stacked. It's a fixed fight.

> We battle, but with one difference: we win. It's a fixed fight.

Now that we have our armor on, the time has come to go to war. Don't let that scare you, brave warriors. We are more than conquerors. We saw with our own eyes overwhelming victory is ours. Overwhelming? You better believe it!

How do we gain overwhelming victory? What must we do? It's come down to the wire. There's no more time to prepare. The clock has struck the hour and the battle is at hand. It's time to face the enemy. Don't get frightened now. This will be interesting if not enjoyable.

Wait. Battle enjoyable? Stick with me here.

When you step into church, what is the first activity (after announcements of course)? Worship. We begin our service with praise and worship to the Lord. Many people may think worship is the entertainment before the preaching. It's not. It is the battle cry. Worship is the song that gets the attention of the Father. He is listening. He is waiting. Waiting for what? For you to give Him the open door to fight your battle. You simply need to take your place and stand firm.

There is someone else listening too, dear warrior. The enemy is also listening. He hears, too. He's watching. He's also angry because he knows he is already defeated. He couldn't scare you. He couldn't intimidate you. He couldn't confuse you because you made the decision to put your focus on the Lord and worship Him. Worship, dear warriors, worship the Lord before you go into battle because...

Worship is warfare.

When you begin to sing, to worship God, amazing things start happening. God responds to your sincere, heartfelt, sometimes fearful, worship. He has done it for our ancestors before us—He will continue to be there for us. He promised.

Do not be afraid or discouraged, for the LORD will personally go ahead of you. He will be with you; he will neither fail you nor abandon you. ~Deuteronomy 31:8, NLT

Notice the first four words: "Do not be afraid." There it is again. God telling us not to be afraid. He also doesn't want us to be discouraged. That can be tough sometimes, especially when our situation appears to be hopeless. We may think God isn't there, but what does the next phrase say? It says that the LORD will personally go ahead of us. That's another promise from God. He will be with us. He will not fail us. He will not abandon us.

In the previous verse there is a hint of a link to your

identity. You are *not alone*. God has promised never to leave you, fail you, or abandon you. Therefore, you are never alone. We can talk about it all day, but the fact remains that even when we feel as if we are alone, we really aren't. So, take courage in that today! That would be an awesome reason to worship Him, don't you think? There were others who thought it best to worship God with singing, too. Let's take a look.

In 2 Chronicles, we find the armies of the Moabites, Ammonites, and some of the Meunites had declared war on Jehoshaphat (pronounced *Yehoshafat*). While that would make anyone terrified, as it did Jehoshaphat, something great was about to happen.

Upon receiving word from messengers that these tribes had declared war against him, Jehoshaphat first went straight to the LORD and begged Him for guidance, and second, he ordered everyone in Judah to begin fasting. Fasting is important when seeking guidance from the Lord. But then Jehoshaphat begins to pray. He stood before the people and prayed, worshiping the Lord God for all He had brought them through thus far, reminding Him of all His blessings and promises.

I met a very special woman several years ago who had a wonderful testimony. She had been given a very disturbing and hopeless diagnosis from her doctor. She was told she had cancer and was not given very many months to live.

The doctors had run some tests, then sent her home to await the results. She went home to be with her family and to enjoy what time she had left. While she was waiting, she received a couple of visitors one day; a woman and her little girl. The youngster was also battling cancer.

As they talked, the little girl looked at the woman and said, "Don't you believe in God?"

"Yes, I do."

"Then why are you acting like you're going to die?"

This profound, yet truthful statement from an innocent but brave child was just what the woman needed.

When her visitors left, the woman went to her favorite comfy chair, grabbed her Bible, and said, "Thank you, Lord, for healing me." She then began looking up every Scripture that talked about healing.

At the next doctor visit the woman had, the doctors were stumped. The test results all came back negative. There was absolutely nothing wrong with this woman! However, she wasn't stumped at all. She knew her God had gone before her and fought her battle for her. All she had to do was worship Him.

In our passage in 2 Chronicles, Jehoshaphat began to honor God, to worship Him by telling Him how great He is and reminding Him of all He had brought the His people through and all His promises to the people. After that, Jehoshaphat said one more thing.

In verse twelve of chapter twenty, Jehoshaphat says, *"O our God, won't you stop them? We are powerless against this mighty army that is about to attack us. We don't know what to do, but we are looking to you for help."*

When you don't know what to do, look to God for help. We really should seek His guidance first, in all things. Even though sometimes we are suddenly presented with a problem, like the woman I mentioned above, and we are so taken aback by it that we just don't know what to do. However, check out what it says in Matthew 6:33 below, from the New Century Version.

"Seek first God's kingdom and what God wants. Then all your other needs will be met as well."

When we look to God first, above all other things, all our other needs will be met. Don't you find that comforting? I certainly do. If we put God first, the things God wants us to do, He will meet our needs.

In 2 Chronicles 20, I find it awesome and amazing that after the people have all fasted, the king has prayed, asking for the Lord's guidance, telling Him they don't know what to do, that God sends a message through one of the men standing with all the people, wives, little ones (meaning babies) and children.

Notice, the Spirit of the Lord came upon one of the men. Not the king, but "one of the men" in the community. This shows that God works through any of His people, not just a choice few. Which means, dear warriors, He will work through you, too.

The first thing the LORD said to the people was, "Do not be afraid!"

There it is again. God telling His people not to be afraid. In my Bible there is an exclamation mark after that sentence. Apparently, God thought it greatly important this time that these people know they should not be afraid. He meant what He said.

Let's break down the next statement. After declaring the LORD said don't be afraid, the man (Jahaziel) tells the people, "Don't be discouraged by this mighty army."

God didn't want the people of Judah to be discouraged by the mighty army. There were three armies preparing to go to war on Jehoshaphat and his people. I don't know about you, but I might just be feeling a little intimidated; okay, a whole lot intimidated. However, God is a good, good Father and He knows what's best for His children. If He tells us not to be afraid and not to be discouraged, then we should do our best to listen to Him.

But look at the next phrase in that statement, "...for the battle is not yours, but God's."

It makes more sense when we discover that the battle we are about to face isn't even ours to begin with. The battle belongs to God. *Every* battle belongs to God! But here's where it gets even better. God, through His Holy Spirit, revealed to the people not only how the enemies were going to come against them, but also how they were to fight.

Every battle belongs to God!

They were given prior knowledge. It's like when we play hide-and-seek with our children. When one grownup hides, the other reveals the hiding place to the child so he can win. Well, God isn't hiding, but He sent the Holy Spirit to reveal the enemy plot to the people so they would know what to do to win.

In verse seventeen, the first thing the people were told about the upcoming battle was to march out against the enemy. They were even told where they would find them, where they were coming from, and that they wouldn't even have to fight. However, they were instructed to take three steps: take your positions, stand still, and watch the LORD's victory.

Again, the people were encouraged to not be afraid, not be discouraged, and twice it is mentioned that the Lord would be with them.

Right after receiving this Divine message, what did

Jehoshaphat and the people begin to do? They bowed low with their faces to the ground, worshiping the LORD. King Jehoshaphat stepped forward in leadership by bowing first and the people followed suit. Then, they stood to praise the LORD "with a very loud shout," (2 Chronicles 20:19).

Even before the enemy armies showed up, the people began to worship God. But the next morning is when things got real.

On the way to the battlefield the king stops and begins talking to the people. After he encourages them, he begins sending people out. This is where the war begins. The first ones out were singers, who went out ahead of the army and began singing praises to the LORD. Remember, earlier in the chapter we discussed that worship is warfare.

When the people began singing, it states "at that very moment" (v. 22), the LORD caused the armies to start fighting among themselves, and they killed each other off.

The LORD doesn't kid around when it comes to the battle. We often get ourselves in a tizzy worrying about how we're going to handle things when we don't even have to handle it in the first place. The battle is not ours. It belongs to God and He is more than capable of taking care of things and us. He never loses.

When we have on our full armor and are prayed up, then begin our battle by worshiping God, He finishes the fight even before it begins. This is what we have been leading up to. Not only did the armies of Ammon, Moab, and Mount Seir start fighting amongst themselves, they killed each other. The army of Judah didn't have to do a thing…just like God said.

It's no different for us. When we stand, just as we were told to do, we will still be standing when the battle is over. Sound familiar?

God doesn't stop there, even. Look at 2 Chronicles 20:24:

So when the army of Judah arrived at the lookout point in the wilderness, all they saw were dead bodies lying on the ground as far as they could see. Not a single one of the enemy had escaped.

When the army of Judah arrived at the lookout point, all they found were dead bodies? Absolutely. When King Jehoshaphat and his men went out to gather the plunder, they found large amounts of equipment, clothing, and other valuables. The Word says, *more than they could carry* (v. 25).

They didn't have to fight. They were to worship the LORD first, then stand still and watch God fight for them, and after it was all over with they even got rewarded? Yes! They were given the possessions of the enemy. All of it!

Oh, mighty warriors, do you not see that even today your fight is fixed? You win! Just like the people with Jehoshaphat were given victory over their enemies, so have you.

You may be wondering if this even applies to our lives today. It does. We may not come against huge armies as the people of Judah did, but we still have war declared on us emotionally, mentally and spiritually. Sometimes it even gets physical and that often changes the battle plan. We have discussed that periodically throughout this study. Yet, God never meant for us to live in a state of fear, but to stand boldly, praising Him and let Him fight our battles no matter how small or insignificant we think they may be. If it's important to you, it's important to God because you are His child and He adores you.

Worship is Warfare
Part Two: There's a Time to Run

Every good soldier knows when to stand and when to run. When the troops deploy, they have times when they stay still. They don't move. Yet they are in battle. However, when the C.O. (Commanding Officer) gives the order, the troops advance. They run forward, at the enemy, fully armored, fully prepared, straight into battle.

While we've studied being bold and standing firm against our enemy, knowing all we need to do is stand still and let God fight our battles, there comes a time when we do need to run. However, that does not mean we run in retreat. The time will come when we must run *at* the enemy. Toward. Sword raised. Shield up. Battle cry on our lips.

Run at the enemy.

Let's face it, we live in hostile times. We always have. This world is not our home. Yet, we are placed here for a time and purpose known only to God. He has a reason and purpose for having you and me in this time period. We were chosen for here and now. *We* are the ones who are capable, through Him, of handling the battles before us.

Yes, we will have times when we do stand and watch the LORD fight for us. Other times, He will tell us to run at the enemy. It will be during that time when God makes a show that will impact many and may just change your life in the process. But how will we know whether to stand or to run? By having faith in the Lord and asking Him for guidance, then doing what the Holy Spirit tells us to do.

In 1 Samuel 17, we see the Philistines have gathered their army for battle against Israel. Yet another battle looms with

God's people and their enemy. As Saul gathered the Israelite troops on one hill, the Philistine troops gathered on the other hill with the valley in between (1 Samuel 17:1-3).

There is quite a difference in this scenario than from the one we read about in 2 Chronicles. In 1 Samuel 16, Samuel had been instructed by God to anoint David to become the next king of Israel. David then found favor with Saul, the current king, and was serving the king as his armor bearer while still also tending his father's sheep.

It was during this time when the Philistines had come against Israel. The enemy stands on a hill, ready to strike and the people don't know what to do. They are being intimidated by the enemy; mocked, ridiculed, laughed at. Little do they know, things are about to change for everyone, including David.

As the Israelites and Philistines are in a stand-off, Goliath steps out and begins taunting the Israelite army. The Bible describes Goliath as over nine feet tall. His armor is described as a bronze helmet, a bronze coat of mail which weighed 125 pounds. He also wore bronze leg armor and carried a bronze javelin on his shoulder. His spear is described as being heavy and thick as a beam, tipped with an iron spearhead which weighed fifteen pounds, and his armor bearer walked ahead of him carrying a shield.

I don't know about you, but if a man who was over nine feet tall stepped out from the ranks of the enemy's army, I think I might be *more* than a little bit intimidated! It wasn't bad enough that this giant of a man steps out from the ranks of the troops, he then begins taunting the Israelites.

In 1 Samuel 17:8-10, the taunts Goliath begins calling out are, *"Why are you all coming out to fight? I am the Philistine champion, but you are only servants of Saul. Choose one man to come down here and fight me! If he kills me, then we will be your slaves. But if I kill him, you will be our slaves! I defy the armies of Israel today! Send me a man who will fight me!"*

When Saul and the Israelites heard these things, they were terrified and deeply shaken (v. 11). This went on for forty days!

Dear Warriors, these are the very same things you and I come against every day. While they may not sound exactly like what Goliath said to Saul and the Israelites, they are threats, taunts, and intimidation nonetheless. And, just like our ancestors before us, we often react the very same way: terrified and deeply shaken.

Can you imagine being taunted by the enemy for forty days? Some people have been taunted and terrified by the enemy (the devil) longer than that. Not everyone knows they are under enemy attack. They believe they were either born that way, inherited their condition, or some even believe they actually did something to cause themselves to be in the situation they are in. Some people believe that God is punishing them and they deserve to be miserable. Not true.

Oh, but friends, things are about to change.

So humble yourselves before God. Resist the devil, and he will flee from you.
Come close to God, and God will come close to you.
~James 4:7-8a, NLT

The first thing we need to do is to humble ourselves before God. Next, we are to resist the devil. When we do, we are told he will flee from us. But then we are told that if we come close to God, He will come close to us. That should be so comforting to us!

God is always waiting for us. He won't invade our lives, because He is a gentleman. Yet, He loves us too much to leave us alone. While the Israelites are cowering before their enemy, someone comes along and decides enough is enough.

David begins asking the members of the Israelite army not only what the reward would be for killing their enemy, but I believe he was beginning to feel righteous anger. Not self-righteous anger, but righteous anger. There's a difference.

David became angry because the Philistine was defying *the armies of the living God*. He wanted to know, just who did Goliath think he was, coming against the armies of the living God? Apparently, the Israelite army had forgotten who they were, too. But read that last part from verse twenty-six: *"Who is this pagan Philistine anyway, that he is allowed to defy the armies of the living God?"*

If you look at the end of that sentence, you will discover another link to your identity. Not only were the Israelites God's people, so are we. Therefore, as His sons and daughters, His warriors, we are **part of the armies of the living God** as well.

Maybe you don't feel like you're part of an army. But if you've come this far in this study, you can bank on this fact. Not only are you all those words you've been writing on that page in the back of the book, you are also one of God's troops. You are a **warrior**! Write that one down in all capital letters on that special identity page and be proud of it because as a WARRIOR you are also **undefeated**.

Let's move on…

David has begun asking questions, looking for information regarding the demise of this enemy who is taunting the armies of the living God. The armies have forgotten who they are. They have forgotten their identity. Even Saul has fallen victim to the taunts and believes they are already defeated.

Yet, although the Israelites believe there is no hope, what does David says to them, "Don't worry about this Philistine, I'll go fight him!" (v 32).

David is doing something that the Israelites should have been doing all along. He's putting his faith in God for victory. He's standing firm in his faith. He's believing God. He's walking boldly and confidently, declaring *out of his mouth* that he will fight the Philistine and win (vv. 34-37).

But, you know, whenever we step out in faith to do what the Lord has called us to do, there will be those who rise up to prevent us from moving forward as we've been called. They will try to change us, give us their advice, discourage us and often times stand in our way to prevent us from completing the task we know we're supposed to accomplish.

Saul had told David not to be ridiculous and that there was no way he (David) could possibly win against Goliath (see verses 38-39). But David persisted, explaining to King Saul how he protected his father's sheep and killed both lion and bear. Defeating a Philistine giant wouldn't be a problem. He was that confident.

Therefore, Saul consented, but decided David needed armor and gave him his own to wear. David put it on, but he knew it wouldn't work because he had never worn such armor before, and it was made for Saul, not David, so it wasn't a right fit. This could be a good lesson for us today.

We can't wear someone else's armor any more than we can be like someone else. We can try, but it's never a right fit. We are all made to be unique. Therefore, we should all be ourselves and operate in the gifts God has given each of us specifically. I can't walk your walk and you can't walk mine. But we can come alongside one another and spur each other on, encourage one another, and help each other when we need help.

"For you are a holy people to the LORD your God, and the LORD has chosen you to be a people for Himself, a special treasure above all the peoples who are on the face of the earth."
~Deuteronomy 14:2, NKJV

Wow! Would you like to talk about who you are now? There are so many links to your identity in this one verse. We have already discovered we are chosen. But look at all those identity markers. O Mighty Warriors, you are a ***holy people*** to God. You are chosen to be someone just for Him. Think about this for a minute; it says the LORD chose you to be a people for Himself. You have been ***hand-picked***. That's another link. It goes on to say that you are also a ***special treasure***. How humbling is this to know God personally hand-picked each one of us to be a special treasure to Himself? I can hardly contain it. Oh, don't stop there. Immediately after we discover we are a special treasure it says we are *"above all the peoples who are on the face of the earth."* Did you catch that? We are ***above***, not beneath. Hard to take it all in? I understand.

"And the LORD will make you the head and not the tail; you shall be above only, and not beneath, if you heed the commandments of the LORD your God, which I command you today, and are careful to observe them."
~Deuteronomy 28:13, NKJV

In this astounding verse you find more links to your identity. Not only does it confirm that you are *above and not beneath*, you are also *the head and not the tail.* This simply means that if we follow what God has told us to do or not to do, we will be in front, not behind. He will elevate us. He will prosper us. He will more than take care of us if we simply follow Him.

Looking back at David, now we can see how important it was to him that someone stand up to the Philistine enemy who was making snide remarks about God. David was about to do what the Israelite armies wouldn't, or maybe couldn't.

As he prepares to go to battle with Goliath, David not only took off Saul's armor, which didn't fit, he only chose five smooth stones from a stream and put those in his bag. As he walked out across the valley, the only thing he was armed with was his shepherd's staff and his sling (v. 40).

Now, as with any big bully, of course Goliath is going to continue to taunt, even curse David. David replies to Goliath's taunts. He boldly declares exactly how and by Whom he is going to come against this enemy. He even tells him how he is going to kill him.

Goliath had been defying God and his people for forty days. As David started across the valley to face off with his enemy, the last thing he said to the Philistine was the promise God had given to the people long ago.

"This is the LORD's battle, and He will give you to us!"
~1 Samuel 17:47b, NLT

And as Goliath moved to attack, David ran at the enemy (v. 48).

There *is* a time to run; a time to run at your enemy. Though we discussed in Part One of this chapter the importance of standing still and watching God fight our battles, there comes a time when we must run at our enemy.

Run at depression.

Run at anxiety.

Run at bi-polar.

Run at cancer.

Run at all disease.

Run at all oppression.

Run.

Run, O Mighty Warrior.

RUN!

Draw your sword and run!

You are promised overwhelming victory. You are promised you will be more than a conqueror. Do you know what it means to be *more* than a conqueror?

David defeated Goliath that day. He not only knocked his enemy down with a sling and one stone, he killed that over-nine-foot-tall giant with the giant's own sword and cut off the giant's head. Can I get an "Amen!" Not just that, but here is where David became more than a conqueror: he killed Goliath, cut off his head to prove he had defeated this Philistine who had come against the living God, and kept all of Goliath's armor. David was rewarded for conquering the enemy. That is what being more than a conqueror is. We not only win, we receive the rewards.

Once David killed Goliath and the Philistines saw it, they turned and ran. This gave the Israelites enough courage to finally take a stand and run at their enemies as well…and they won.

When we take a stand against our enemy, when we declare God openly with our mouths and trust Him for victory, we will be victorious. Not only that but our enemies will turn and run when they see our victory.

There's no need to fear *any* battle. There will be no casualties. However, you must understand, if we do nothing, if we never give God the glory, never worship Him, if we never stand, if we never run at the enemy, the battle will never be fought and we will remain captives in whatever is holding us down. We, as Mighty Warriors, must stand. We must take our place in God's army. We must fight the battle, which means either standing firm on God's promise of overwhelming victory and watching Him fight our battle for us while we sing His praises, or running at the enemy and allowing God to fight through us to win the battle.

> There's no need to fear any battle.

Whatever the battle plan, we win because, remember, the fight is fixed. We are guaranteed victory. We just need to make up our mind to accept that victory on behalf of our good, good Father.

Debriefing:

We have discovered many links to our identity in this chapter. We learned that worship is warfare. Singing praises to God begins the battle. We do not battle alone. We have learned that sometimes we stand and watch God fight for us, but sometimes it is necessary to run at our enemy. Possibly the most important thing we've learned is that the battle is not ours but the Lord's. Our fight is also fixed because we win. We win because God wins and He never loses.

Be sure to write all the links you found in both sections of this chapter on the **Who I Am in Christ** *page.*

Further Reading:
2 Chronicles 20:1-30
1 Samuel 16-17

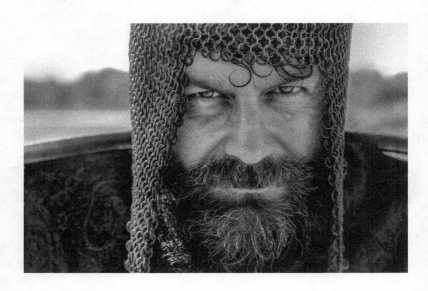

7 Arise, O Mighty Warrior!

"The great need of the present hour is Christians who have learned to sing the song of deliverance on the testing side of trouble."

~David Wilkerson, "Right Song, Wrong Side" sermon
(2009)

We have talked about so much throughout the last few chapters. It can be a bit overwhelming, if not intimidating, when discovering who we really are and who we were meant to be. One thing is certain: God definitely has great big plans for you and me, dear friend. He has always had good plans for us because He is our good, good Father. What parent doesn't want the best for their children?

However, even though we know God is always there for us, we must remember we can't just sit idly by and expect Him to do everything for us. It doesn't work that way. We have to get up, arise, and take our place as we were designed to do. We must be obedient to the call we have on our lives.

Still not sure of your identity? Not sure you are cut out to be a warrior, much less a mighty one? Maybe it hasn't sunk in just yet. That's okay. Sometimes it takes a bit for the truth to sink in. Sometimes we need confirmation, after confirmation, after confirmation. There were several people in the Bible who also needed confirmation, affirmation, realization, and many other "*tions*."

One particular person comes to mind. In the book of Judges, a man named Gideon discovered much about himself in a short amount of time.

Read Judges 6:11-12 below from The Message.

"One day the angel of GOD came and sat down under the oak in the Ophrah that belonged to Joash the Abiezrite, whose son Gideon was threshing wheat in the winepress, out of sight of the Midianites.

The angel of GOD appeared to him and said, "GOD is with you, O mighty warrior!"

Here we have dear Gideon, hiding from the Midianites and threshing wheat in the winepress so maybe his people can get a little grain and not have it stolen out from under them like they've had done the last few years (see Judges 6:1-10). While he's hiding, hidden from the enemy, the angel of GOD just appears to him? Then calls him "O Mighty Warrior?"

Absolutely!

Now read verse thirteen below.

Gideon replied, "With me, my master? If GOD is with us, why has all this happened to us? Where are all the miracle-wonders our parents and grandparents told us about, telling us, 'Didn't GOD deliver us from Egypt?' The fact is, GOD has nothing to do with us–he has turned us over to Midian.

Gideon responds with a little doubt, don't you think? I'm not sure but, if an angel appeared to me while I was hiding from my enemies and called me a mighty warrior, I don't know that I would believe him, either. But isn't this how most of us respond to something God says to us?

Yet, even though Gideon was hesitant to believe his identity, he wasn't at all afraid to ask why all this stuff was happening to them when he thought his people were supposed to have been delivered. Read on.

But GOD faced him directly: "Go in this strength that is yours. Save Israel from Midian. Haven't I just sent you?"
~Judges 6:14, The Message

Do you see how it suddenly changes from "an angel of GOD" to simply "GOD?" For just a moment, I want you to look back at the passage. Notice how GOD is written in all capital letters? In the NKJV the word is LORD. Again, all caps. The reference to GOD is the same as LORD. Remember in the beginning of this book, I referenced the different spellings and the meaning of the Lord's name? When written in all caps, regardless of GOD or LORD, this is the Hebrew transliteration

YHWH, emphasizing His position as covenant maker and keeper.

We are about to see something amazing, Warriors! Keep going!

The LORD addressed Gideon by his identity as HE saw him: "O mighty warrior!" He also sees you as you are in Christ. Do you not yet see yourself that way? My dear friends in Christ, here is possibly the most powerful link to your identity: *mighty warrior*.

There are times when even I don't feel mighty, much less a warrior. Forget it. Lord, I'm not mighty, nor a warrior so please don't put them together and call me a mighty warrior! Yet, that's exactly who I am! That's who you are! Believe it, because it's true.

Yes, we are currently reading about Gideon. However, this could very well be your story. It sure used to be mine. Maybe you're hiding out, trying your best not to be seen by anyone, enemy or otherwise. You just want to quietly exist, no attention brought your way, don't anyone notice me, address me, or ask me to be part of anything. Especially don't ask me about my situation or things I've been through or done. I would be mortified. Is that you?

I've been there. So deep in depression I can't see daylight even though the sun is shining brightly. I've been intimidated by everyone who looks at me, so embarrassed thinking someone might say something to me about some stupid thing I did, or which they perceive that I did and then I would have to defend myself. I've been so intimidated knowing that no one is going to believe a word I say and embarrassed they are going to cause me trouble that I avoid even speaking to anyone. Worse yet, I open my mouth and say all the wrong things and ruin any witness I may have had for the Lord because I just wanted to cause people to back away from me so I didn't have to associate with anyone. Yes, friends, I've been there.

But that is* not *who I was, nor is it who I am today.

Neither is it who *you* are. We have come so very far in this book of discovering our identity in Christ; who we are in Him, who He says we are. Now is the time to arise, O Mighty Warrior. Now is the time to take your place in God's mighty army, because you have been called, appointed, chosen, anointed, gifted, and challenged. You have a mighty call on your life to rescue those who are where you once were.

Because God healed me of depression, anxiety, intimidation, and verbal and emotional abuse, my call is to help rescue and encourage those who are suffering in the same things. Your call may be similar or it may be different.

Maybe you are recovering from alcohol or substance abuse. Rescue those who are where you once were.

Maybe you were once a victim of sexual abuse. Rescue those who are where you once were.

Maybe you were once addicted to pornography. Rescue those who are where you once were.

Maybe you were once a victim of domestic violence. Rescue those who are where you once were.

Maybe you were once addicted to gambling. Rescue those who are where you once were.

The list is endless, my friends. Whatever you are going through, there is someone or several someones who are going through the same things you once struggled with. Your call is to help rescue them and show them the Love of Jesus. You may be the only Jesus they see because no one else will hold their hand out to them to lift them out of the pit they are in.

You know, when the LORD (all capital letters) addressed Gideon as "mighty warrior," Gideon wasn't quite sure how to take that. He asked the Lord about it. This is where I find such encouragement. Whenever the Lord gives us instructions, if we don't understand, we absolutely *can* ask Him questions and He will help us understand. In other words, it is okay to ask "why?" provided we don't question His authority. Simply ask for wisdom in understanding what He just told you.

So he said to Him, "O my Lord, how can I save Israel? Indeed my clan is the weakest in Manasseh, and I am the least in my father's house."

And the LORD said to him, "Surely I will be with you, and you shall defeat the Midianites as one man."

~Judges 6:15-16, NKJV

Gideon was a bit confused as to how he was supposed to save an entire nation (Israel), from such a huge army of enemies. His clan was small, he (Gideon) was small, and he just couldn't wrap his mind around what he was being told. So, he asked questions.

But the LORD tells Gideon that He will be with him, and that he will also be victorious.

Maybe you're a bit confused about your role, your calling. I admit, it can be a little intimidating, especially when you've never done anything like that before, or even if you never thought you would or could be of much use to the Lord. However, if the Lord says He will be with you, you can believe what He says. He never lies and He always comes through on His Word.

Let's look a little deeper at that conversation. Watch the

spelling. Gideon addresses Him as Lord. However, when He answers back to Gideon, the Bible addresses Him as LORD (all caps).

This is intentional. Gideon acknowledges the Lord in His position as Master. Even though he isn't certain at this point exactly Who he is conversing with, he still has the presence of mind to know he is in the presence of someone holy. Therefore, he addresses Him as Lord; lower case letters, emphasizing lordship and position as Master.

When the LORD answers Gideon, He was already announcing the covenant with him and that He was Gideon's keeper, meaning no harm would come to Gideon or his people.

I find this exceptionally profound. How many people did not know this would be written in God's Word one day? Yet here it is for you and me to know and to learn and ponder the magnitude of how far God will go to rescue His people, but also to let us know exactly Who He is to us at that moment.

However, it's also understandable to be slightly confused about *how* He will do what He says. Nevertheless, Gideon still asks… and the Lord, ever so patient, answers him.

> *Gideon said, "If you're serious about this, do me a favor: Give me a sign to back up what you're telling me. Don't leave until I come back and bring you my gift."*
> *He said, "I'll wait till you get back."*
> ~Judges 6:17-18 (I used The Message here)

Even though the Lord had said He would be with Gideon and that he would defeat the Midianites as though he were one man, Gideon asks the Lord for a sign and the Lord tells him He will wait.

Isn't that just like us today? God gives us instructions, encouragement, and we ask for a sign to be sure it's true. Yet, He is so patient, loving and kind! He *waited*.

In Gideon's day, it was proper to bring an offering to the Lord, as Gideon did. He prepared and brought a young goat, unraised bread, and broth in a pot. When he presented it to the angel of God something miraculous happened. The angel of GOD told Gideon to take the meat and unraised bread, place them on a rock and pour the broth on them. Then he stretched out the tip of the stick he was holding, touched the meat and the bread, and fire broke out of the rock and burned up everything. And the angel of God slipped away while this took place.

In the words of Bill Engvall, *"Here's your sign!"* What more could a person want? Here, Gideon brings this food and broth as his offering to the Lord. He places the bread and meat on the rock and is told to pour the broth over the offering. Now it's wet. We all know wet things don't burn. But as the angel of the LORD stretches out the tip of the stick and touches the bread and meat, fire breaks out of the rock and burns up everything! Gideon now knew *Who* he had seen and had been talking to... and comes completely undone. I think that would have me shaking in my mismatched socks, too.

While Gideon is having his moment, the Lord speaks again.

But GOD reassured him, "Easy now. Don't panic. You won't die." ~Judges 6:23, The Message

I love how The Message Bible puts things in such down-to-earth verbiage. The first thing the LORD does is tell Gideon to calm down then reassures him that he won't die. "You're not going to die. I just told you you're a mighty warrior and are going to defeat this huge army as if you were one man."

Why would God take him out of the equation when God just hold him he was about to do something amazing? Let's look at it another way; Why would God take *you* out of the equation when He just told you you're about to do something amazing? Yet, isn't this exactly how we think today? We automatically begin thinking negatively, preparing for the worst even though we have a great calling on our lives.

My dear warriors, this is a ploy of the enemy, to whisper lies into our minds and get us to snowball them out of proportion so badly that we cause ourselves to panic. When we overreact to the enemy's lies, we put the brakes on the Lord's plans. We inadvertently slow our own progress because of fear, uncertainty, panic, indecisiveness, and just blatant disobedience.

Yet, even when we realize what we've done, the enemy loves to instill fear in us that the Lord is mad at us and going to *zap* us into oblivion. He instills in us false fears to prevent us from coming boldly to God and allowing Him to bring us back into a right relationship with Him. That's how we find so many today who truly believe God can't use them anymore, if ever. We find our brothers (and even sisters) in Christ in a proverbial spiritual fetal position, unable to move, much less utter the words needed to engage the Holy Spirit for help. They have allowed the lies of the enemy to stop them in their tracks and cause them to believe their life is over.

But God's Word says otherwise. Look at Psalm 118:17 from the New King James Version below.

"I shall not die, but live, And declare the works of the LORD."

Just as the Angel of GOD spoke to Gideon and told him he would not die; the first part of the above verse assure us the same thing. We will not die but live. Instead, we will declare the works of the LORD.

Again, if God has saved you, called you, anointed you, appointed you and chosen you (remember writing all these links?) do you really think He is going to allow you to die before you walk out your assignment? *NO!*

You shall not die, but live!

It's very easy to become confused about what might happen when God gives you an assignment. Let's remember that the enemy wants us to be confused. He wants us to fail. Therefore, he will plant obstacles in our way to prevent us from being victorious.

In Judges 6:24-32 the LORD gave Gideon an assignment. Gideon carried it out, but did it at night because "he was afraid of the other members of his father's household and the people of the town," (v. 27). It wasn't until the next morning that the people discovered the altar of Baal had been torn down and the Asherah pole beside it had been cut down. They discovered a new altar that had been built and the remains of a sacrifice— and they were angry. So angry that they went to great lengths to find out who had done it and wanted Gideon put to death.

Know this: There will always be someone or something that stands in your way. However, when you are obedient to what the LORD tells you to do, great things begin to happen.

Soon afterward the armies of Midian, Amalek, and the people of the east formed an alliance against Israel and crossed the Jordan, camping in the valley of Jezreel. Then the Spirit of the LORD clothed Gideon with power. *He blew a ram's horn as a call to arms, and the men of the clan of Abiezer came to him. He also sent messengers throughout Manasseh, Asher, Zubulun, and Naphtali, summoning their warriors, and all of them responded.*

~Judges 6:33-35, NLT (emphasis is mine).

Although the people were angry with Gideon for destroying their idols, God blessed Gideon. The Spirit of the LORD came upon Gideon and when he blew the trumpet (the ram's horn), people came from all around to gather. Remember, there was an army against them. These people had been living in fear, being bullied and enslaved by their enemies the Midianites.

The Israelites were in slavery once again because of their disobedience to God (remember the altar to Baal and the Asherah pole?). For *seven years* they were in bondage. However, when they cried out to the LORD, He heard them and God raised up a deliverer to bring them out of bondage once again. This is where we find our story.

The Spirit of the LORD (the Holy Spirit) had come upon Gideon and now he was gathering the troops, preparing to take on the enemy. But God begins to thin out the numbers. This may sound ludicrous to us; to be called to stand against your enemy, only to have God thin out the number of troops before they even go to battle? Yet God has a plan and a purpose and it is always for the good.

In Judges chapter seven, God thins the Israelite troops from twenty-two thousand men down to a mere three hundred to defeat the Midianites. Why was this so important?

And the LORD said to Gideon, "The people who are with you are too many for Me to give the Midianites into their hands, lest Israel claim glory for itself against Me, saying, 'My own hand has saved me.'" ~Judges 7:2, NKJV

The reason the LORD told Gideon there were too many people for Him (God) to give the Midianites over to the Israelites was so they didn't take the credit for their victory. We often think how ridiculous for God to do that, but is there any time in your own life when you might have wanted to take credit for something you know God has done through you? I know I have.

When God gives an assignment, He will provide the way and means for you to be successful. If we look back on the last chapter, we either stand and watch the LORD fight *for* us, or we run at the enemy and allow Him to

> When God gives an assignment, He will provide the way and means for you to be successful.

defeat said enemy *through* us. Remember, our fight is fixed. We win. No matter what. All we have to do is be obedient to our calling.

Gideon was obedient and lived. His people lived. Their enemy? They died. How? Just as the LORD told Gideon they would. Now remember, a lot of things happened in between, but I want to focus on the actual event. Gideon was in fact obedient to what the LORD told him to do. In doing so, victory was won.

Yet, even in our victory, the victory is not ours but belongs to God. It's not about us. The fight isn't even ours. The fight belongs to God. Therefore, if we take credit for the victory, even though we were the ones who conquered, we are doing God a great disservice. It's not about us. It's all about God.

I know it must sound like a catch-22 statement, but it's not. We are all part of God's historic and amazing plan. We have no idea the magnitude of our role in His work. We just need to remember that His ways are much higher than ours. His thoughts are much greater than we can imagine. But one day we will know and, when we do, what a glorious revelation we will behold!

Throughout this story, we saw a warrior rise up. My dear siblings in Christ, you are also a warrior. It is time that you, as well, rise up. You *will* be victorious. You *will* conquer. You *will* overcome, because this is who you are. This is what you were born to do. You are living in the time you're meant to live in. You were designed to do the things you do in this life. And you are promised victory.

Make no mistake, dear friends; if you do nothing, the battle will not be won. People will not be set free. You will not advance in your spiritual walk. You will never win the victory if you don't arise, O Mighty Warrior!

You cannot advance if you are continually living in the past, continually waiting for the Lord to move. He *is* moving. He is always moving. But He is waiting on you. Dear warriors, I have watched in sadness, listening to men and women talk about knowing they have a call on their lives yet sit, waiting and watching to see what the Lord is going to do. One of the most frustrating statements I've heard repeatedly is, "I can't wait to see what the Lord is going to do!"

Friends, He is doing stuff *right now*. God is a right now God. He has given the instructions. He is waiting for his Mighty Warriors to arise *now*. God has sent the Holy Spirit to guide us, to lead us, to teach us, and to deliver us. The Holy Spirit is so much more than we allow Him to be simply because we won't move.

Stop waiting. Start moving. Don't let the enemy keep you idle one minute longer.

"Pay attention, my people. Listen to me, nations. Revelation flows from me. My decisions light up the world. My deliverance arrives on the run, my salvation right on time. I'll bring justice to the people. Even faraway islands will look to me and take hope in my saving power. Look up at the skies, ponder the earth under your feet. The skies will fade out like smoke, the earth will wear out like work pants, and the people will die off like flies. But my salvation will last forever, my setting-things-right will never be obsolete.

"Listen now, you who know right from wrong, you who hold my teaching inside you:

"Pay no attention to insults, and when mocked don't let it get you down. Those insults and mockeries are moth-eaten, from brains that are termite-ridden, But my setting-things-right lasts, my salvation goes on and on and on."

~Isaiah 51:4-8, The Message

What does He say comes from Him? Revelation! Deliverance, salvation, justice, saving power, His setting-things-right. When does He say His deliverance and salvation come? His deliverance comes on the run. His salvation comes right on time…and it keeps going on and on and on. Therefore, if we want to know anything, we must seek the LORD, our Covenant Maker and Keeper. He never breaks His covenant with His people. He is always right on time.

Looking at Gideon, remember, after he tore down the idols, what happened the next morning? He had people come against him. We will have that as well, but God has something to say about those who mock us and insult us.

From the passage above, God's Word says to pay no attention to insults. When we are mocked, don't let it get you down.

Sometimes it's easier said than done when it comes to not letting the words of others get us down. We have to remember who we are and Whose we are and then we can stand with confidence, knowing that His deliverance and salvation will come right on time, as always.

Let's not stop there, warriors.

"I, even I, am He who comforts you. Who are you that you should be afraid of a man who will die, and of the son of a man who will be made like grass?

"The captive exile hastens, that he may be loosed, that he should not die in the pit, And that his bread should not fail."

~Isaiah 51:12, 14 (I used NKJV for this passage)

Even in our fear sometimes, we forget the LORD. The Lord comforts us with the shadow of His hand, (read vv. 12-23 to get the entire story).

The captive wants to be set free. Those who are in bondage to one thing or another don't want to be there. Those who suffer depression never planned on having it. Those who are addicted to alcohol or drugs didn't plan to get in that situation. The one who sneaks into the night to view pornography didn't plan to do those things. The one who feels enslaved in a physically abusive relationship never planned for that to happen.

None of the people in these situations ever planned to be where they are. Yet, they are. Many of them don't know how to get free from their captivity. They may be fearful for not only themselves but for others who may be involved. This is how the enemy adds chain link after chain link to the bondage we suffer. We see no way out, therefore not only are we held bound by the chains of our infirmity, regardless of what it is, we also feel hopeless that we will ever see freedom from our situation.

But God has other plans; not only for them but for you. You, dear warriors, have the answer that someone somewhere needs. How do I know? Look at Isaiah 51:16 from the New King James Version, below.

"And I have put My words in your mouth; I have covered you with the shadow of My hand, That I may plant the heavens, Lay the foundations of the earth, And say to Zion, 'You are My people.'"

In the first sentence of that passage, the LORD says He has put His words in our mouths.

We don't have to worry about what to say. He has already put the right words in our mouths; *His* words. All we have to do is be willing to stand up and speak. But that isn't all He has done for you and me.

In verse sixteen, He says, *"I have covered you with the shadow of My hand..."*

Wow! Being covered with the shadow of His hand, do you

not realize that you are being protected? We have just uncovered another link to our identity. We are **covered** (protected) by His hand. His personal hand. The LORD personally covers us. Isn't that enough to spur you on, give you encouragement, excite you into moving forward, or make you throw your hands in the air in praise to Him?

He has explained in the last part of verse sixteen the reason He put His words in our mouth and covered us in the shadow of His hand. Here, again, is His promise:

"That I may plant the heavens, lay the foundations of the earth, and say to Zion, 'You are *My people.'"*

What encouragement! Look at that last statement. There lies another link to your identity. You *Are **His people***. You can literally claim, ***"I am God's people."*** You are HIS.

Having said that, if we look at the rest of the passage, we will find even more ways He sets the captives free. Though we are attacked by the enemy, the LORD is going to turn the tables on those who oppress us.

Look below. The LORD has something to say to you.

Therefore please hear this, you afflicted, And drunk but not with wine.

Thus says your Lord, the LORD and your God, *Who pleads the cause of His people: "See, I have taken out of your hand The cup of trembling, The dregs of the cup of My fury; You shall no longer drink it.*

But I will put it into the hand of those who afflict you, Who have said to you, 'Lie down, that we may walk over you.' And you have laid your body like the ground, And as the street, for those who walk over."

~Isaiah 51:21-23 (emphasis is mine)

There is a very important message within this passage. The LORD wants to make it clear to you and me the seriousness of what He is about to do. I have emphasized it purposely so you would notice.

There are many people who simply cannot wrap their minds around the fact that God doesn't want to harm them but, rather, to free them. They cannot understand that He loves them unconditionally. They can't understand much less believe that He has great plans for them and that they are somebody in and for the kingdom of God.

Maybe, instead of looking at who *we* are, we need to look closer at Who *HE* is. In the beginning of this study, I made reference to the different ways God acknowledges Himself, but we need to look a bit closer at that in this passage. So, let's break it down as He has given us all three descriptions in this one verse alone! I have written them all out individually with their descriptions below then we will break them down separately.

In the passage above, it begins with, *Thus says your Lord.*

Lord. The Hebrew transliteration is a form of *Adonai,* emphasizing God's lordship and His position as Master.

Next in the same sentence is, *The LORD...*

LORD (in all caps). The Hebrew *YHWH* (Yahweh) emphasizes His position as covenant maker and keeper.

Finishing the sentence is, *and your God.*

God. When you see references to *God,* the Hebrew *Elohim* emphasizes His position as universal Creator.

I find this exceptionally profound that He addresses those who are oppressed, those who are going through a rough time, those who feel put down, beat down, held captive, dealing with depression, oppression, addiction, or anything and everything that prevents them from having a relationship with a loving God

Who is crazy about them. That includes you and me.

First, He speaks as Lord. *Your Lord.* He's yours. He's mine. Our Lord, Adonai, the One who is above all. He is Lord of all. Master. Our Master. The LORD. Our LORD. Our Covenant maker and keeper. Our God. Elohim. Our universal Creator.

He is the First, Middle, and Last, surrounding everything and everyone. He even pleads our case; He prays for each and every one of us. No matter what we have been through, Jesus intercedes on our behalf to the Father. He is our High Priest.

Do you see how we cannot fail? Do you see now how the fight is fixed? We win, dear warriors! I don't mind saying it over and over again.

Therefore, there is no reason we cannot arise and be victorious.

For thus says the LORD:
*"You have sold yourselves for nothing, And you shall be redeemed without money." ~*Isaiah 52:3, NKJV

There is yet another link to your identity. You are **redeemed**. Did you see His position?

We aren't finished yet. Being the Mighty Warrior of the LORD (covenant maker and keeper), He also sees us in a wonderful way.

*How beautiful upon the mountains Are the feet of him who brings good news, Who proclaims peace, Who brings glad tidings of good things, Who proclaims salvation, Who says to Zion, "Your God reigns!" ~*Isaiah 52:7, NKJV

Do you see another link to your identity in there? You are

beautiful. Beautiful! He doesn't stop there, though. ***Read for yourself verses 8-10 and be encouraged.***

Before we end this exciting chapter, you must know, dear Mighty Warrior, God adores you. He has set in motion a great series of events all designed to elevate you, prosper you, enlighten you, increase you, and the list is endless of all the possibilities He has for *your* benefit. Yet everything we do should glorify Him or bring glory to Him.

Yes, the enemy means to harm us. He will do everything he can to mess us up. He wants to see us defeated. But what he means for harm, God will turn it for good if we follow His plan and are obedient to the call set upon our lives.

> We must be obedient to the call we have on our lives.

We have been appointed as watchmen for our brothers and sisters in Christ, to help them realize who they are and help rescue them and free them out of the bondage in which they are held captive. Only when we realize that we belong to God, take our stand and voice our position will we be successful.

One last thing I want you to see before we close is that we never have to worry about fighting for the LORD.

For you shall not go out with haste. Nor by flight;
For the LORD will go before you, And the God of Israel will be your rear guard. ~Isaiah 52:12, NKJV

Oh, dear Mighty Warrior, our Yahweh, our covenant maker and keeper goes before us as we go out to battle, and our God, our Elohim, our universal Creator is our rear guard! He leads us and He watches our back!

I am literally in tears as I write this. I cannot fathom the magnitude of it all, yet I am as excited as I can possibly be as I let all this sink in. Not only are we God's special people, we are His anointed, appointed Warriors. His royal children. Royalty!

We cannot be defeated because He is never defeated. We always win because He does. All we have to do is be who He says we are.

So… Who are *you*?

Debriefing:

In this exciting chapter we have discovered it's time to arise as God's Mighty Warriors. Just as Gideon, named a warrior, arose to God's call into battle to save his people, so we must take our place to do likewise. Not only have we discovered more about our identity in Christ, we have also discovered more about who God is as our Lord, Master, covenant maker and keeper, and universal Creator. Knowing this about Him helps us realize that we are never alone and no matter what the enemy throws our way, as long as we know who we are and do what God has called us to do, we will be victorious as well as helping to free others from their oppression.

Don't forget to write the links to your identity on your **Who I Am** *in Christ page in the back.*

Further Reading:
Isaiah 51:12-23
Isaiah 52:7-10

8 Live Free, Live Brave

Freedom is not just freedom from restraint; freedom is freedom to do what God has empowered you to do.
~Mel Lawrenz, Jubilee (2008)

My Dear Mighty Warriors, we have come so very far in our journey of discovering who we are in Christ. Every link we have written down is just a piece in the puzzle of our life's journey. Every link is exactly who God says you are, yet these identifying words are not even one drop in the bucket of eternity to explaining your true identity.

I would encourage you to continue digging through God's Love Letter to you (the Bible) and continue writing down all the beautiful things He says about you. While you're at it, remember that you are free to live as God intended for you to live.

As a Mighty Warrior, you have the freedom to not only live free but live brave. Stand, mighty ones. Take your place among the saints who have gone before you. You haven't earned it. You haven't bought it. It was bought *for* you by the blood of Jesus Christ, Himself and given to all those who ask for it. It is a gift of freedom like none other; one that lasts an eternity.

The enemy will squawk, balk, and cause trouble. Let him. When you know who you are and Whose you are, he cannot touch you. When you put on all your armor and take your stand, using the authority Christ gave you, the enemy can only slink away in defeat. He *is* defeated. He will remain defeated. There is nothing he can do that will turn the tables in his favor. Remember that.

In this chapter we are going to add a little more to our identity. This chapter is dedicated to freedom and bravery, so let's find out what God says about that.

> *"So if the Son sets you free, you are truly free."*
> ~John 8:36, NLT

Who has set us free? Jesus. If the Son, Jesus, has set us free, then we are free. That means from everything: death, hell, addiction, depression, anxiety, abuse, our mistakes, everything. We no longer live in that. We are really, truly, unequivocally free. In that verse is another link to our identity. We are *free*.

Why, then, do we continue to bring up the past mistakes of not only ourselves, but others? Human nature could be a culprit. Many people attribute our words and actions to happenstance. I do not. I suspect a vicious, conniving enemy who slinks and prowls, stalking us, waiting to whisper those lies into our minds then waits for us to let them grow into a slip 'n slide to cause us to slip back into old habits, thoughts, and emotions.

Don't let him do that to you. Don't let anyone do that to you.

We have the very power to turn things around, raise our sword (God's Word) and be overwhelmingly victorious. We have the power to live free and live brave.

Jesus is our Truth and knowing Him sets us free.

A few verses up from the last one we read there lies a very powerful statement.

"Then you will know the truth, and the truth will set you free." ~John 8:32, Berean Study Bible

Jesus is our Truth and knowing Him sets us free. But also knowing His Word will *keep* us free. It's a very profound discovery when you think about it. The more we read the Word, the closer we get to the Lord. The closer we get to the Lord, the more He reveals to us.

Throughout history, the people of God have been enslaved and freed numerous times. In the Old Testament, when the people of God would slide back into sin, old habits, or do what they thought was right instead of what God told them was His plan for them, they would find themselves back in slavery. Many times, God would give them over to their enemies to be held captive for however long it took for them to realize they had done wrong. Sometimes the people would even just sell themselves into slavery thinking it would make things easier on them. It never did.

Don't misunderstand God's actions, however. Though He is loving, fair, just, and righteous, God also does not allow sin. God is perfect. He cannot sin and He cannot lie. He hates those things, but He never hates us. God gives us many opportunities to make a U-turn. He is the God of second, third, fourth, and many more chances. But His patience does run out; especially when His children continue on a downward path, living in sinful ways, doing sinful things and never returning to Him. Often times, He will send someone who can get through to us and help us to see where we strayed. Yet, it is always up to us whether to return to God or continue on our own way.

God freed His people whenever they have cried out to Him. It may have taken a long time in some instances, but God is always on time. He is always working, always setting things up in our favor. Remember in the previous chapter, the fight is fixed—we win. *Always.* As long as we follow God's plan and do what He tells us.

In every passage, we have discussed setting people free because they are enslaved to something. Our enemy, the devil, would like nothing more than to keep us held captive by one means or another. But Jesus came so we could be free, be healed, and live an abundant life. Because of our freedom, we are no longer slaves to the sin by which we were held prisoner.

And remember, if you were a slave when the Lord called you, you are now free in the Lord. And if you were free when the Lord called you, you are now a slave of Christ.
~1 Corinthians 7:22, NLT

Were you a slave when the Lord called you? Think about that for a minute. Was there something that held you captive, preventing you from having a complete relationship with Jesus? Was it depression, anxiety, addiction, abuse, or an illness? Was it worry, un-forgiveness, unbelief, holding a grudge, or something else? What were you doing when you finally felt the Lord tugging on your heart? When you finally turned to Him and asked Him to be your Lord and Savior, He set you free in Him. All those things mentioned above no longer have a stronghold over you.

I must pause right here for one minute. If you have come this far and are still having difficulty identifying with the links to who God says you are, if you are still struggling to come to grips with that, may I ask you a question? Do you truly know Jesus as your Lord and Savior? I don't want you to miss an opportunity to come to know Jesus for the first time, if you have never made Him Lord of your life.

Therefore, I have added an appendix in the back of this book to help you. If you will turn to that page and read through it, I want to give you the opportunity to enter into the most wonderful, loving, rewarding relationship you will ever have. Then come back and finish. We'll wait.

Dictionary.com defines slave as *"a person who is the property of and wholly subject to another; a bondservant."* We can become slaves to many things and even people. But the point of the matter is, whatever you were going through before you came to know the Lord, even before you were freed from whatever troubled you and held you captive, you were a slave to that. All those are things that hold us captive and prevent us from living that abundant life Jesus died to give us.

However, when we come in contact with Jesus, we can never be the same. He changes us. He frees us. Look at the last part of the verse above. To be called by the Lord is great. Once we surrender ourselves to Him, we step into that glorious walk. It doesn't mean our lives will be without trials or events that challenge us. We will have many challenges and battles along the way. But our attitude going into it will determine the outcome. Will we be positive and brave, or allow the negativity to consume us?

Being a slave of Christ doesn't mean we are in bondage again. We are still free. A slave of Christ only means we have become sold out to Him and have risen up and declared our allegiance to Him, our obedience to Him, and will do whatever He has called us to do.

Once we realize we are truly free in Christ, we should be bold in our walk. We should begin walking in the anointing He has poured out on us and run in the calling we have on our lives. Maybe that sounds farfetched, but in truth it is more real that you can possibly know.

However, there are some who never begin to live in the freedom Christ died to give us. Instead, they use their freedom to do whatever they choose to do, blatantly disregarding God's instructions. They make excuses for why they are doing the things they do and living the way they are. These are very dangerous waters, my friends.

Live as people who are free, not using your freedom as a cover-up for evil, but living as servants of God.

~1 Peter 2:6, ESV

How are we supposed to live? As people who are free. Again, being a servant of God, a slave of Christ, only means that we have become so in love with Him that we can't do anything but what He has told us to do. It's not foolish. It's not ridiculous. However, to those who are not living for Him, it is. In fact, it is repulsive.

I think 2 Corinthians 2:14-17 explains it quite well. I've included it below, from the New Living Translation.

But thank God! He has made us his captives and continues to lead us along in Christ's triumphal procession. Now he uses us to spread the knowledge of Christ everywhere, like a sweet perfume.

Our lives are a Christ-like fragrance rising up to God. But this fragrance is perceived differently by those who are being saved and by those who are perishing.

To those who are perishing, we are a dreadful smell of death and doom. But to those who are being saved, we are a life-giving perfume. And who is adequate for such a task as this?

You see, we are not like the many hucksters who preach for personal profit. We preach the word of God with sincerity and with Christ's authority, knowing that God is watching us.

Can you imagine, to people who are perishing—that is, people who are living for themselves and for the world—we are a dreadful smell of death and doom? But to others, those who are living for Jesus, we literally smell like life! We smell like Jesus!

Don't forget, Mighty Warriors, we are in a battle every day. We come in contact with people who are in bondage of one sort or another. Some know it, some do not. Many are looking for a way out and don't know where to turn. Others do not know it, therefore are put off by someone such as yourself who has decided to allow God to heal them and then walk in that healing. You, dear warriors, who have discovered who you are in Christ and have taken the stand to become God's Mighty Warrior can be a help to some…but you're a threat to others.

Your walk will be a threat to someone, or several someones out there who are not living in the grace and mercy of a loving heavenly Father. Instead, they will become negative toward you. These are the ones God may just place in your path for you to rescue. If you remember who you are and Whose you are, you will be victorious.

Remember to stand your ground. Stand for Who you believe in. You never have to be ashamed to stand for Jesus. Instead, you can live free and live brave. Never move or be moved from your faith in Christ.

As we have studied throughout this book, God made a covenant (in the Old Testament) with our ancestors who have gone before us. He is our covenant maker and keeper. He keeps His covenant and never breaks it. In other words, He never goes back on His word and never breaks a promise. In the passage above, we have living proof from the New Testament, through Jesus, that the covenant was fulfilled and a New Covenant put in its place.

You may be asking what that new covenant is. If you'll look back, you will see. God is leading us along *"in Christ's triumphal procession"* and He uses us *"to spread the knowledge of Christ everywhere, like a sweet perfume. "*

Those who know Christ will smell that sweetness on us. Those who do not know Christ, or who are not living for Him, will not smell it. Instead, they will be put off by us.

I know that may sound redundant to some, but as we walk along in our journey, we must remember this so as not to get discouraged and also not think ourselves more highly than we should.

Remember that the Lord will give you an inheritance as your reward, and that the Master you are serving is Christ.
~Colossians 3:24, NLT

It's easy to get sidetracked. However, when we remember Who we serve, the magnitude of our journey becomes even greater.

On the line below, write the identity of the One whom you serve _____

It is a great honor to serve the Lord, to minister to others who suffer in things we have been healed from. It is a great honor and exciting to discover who we are in Christ and then share it with those who haven't realized who they are. Together, we form one powerful force that even the gates of hell can't break.

So, what difference does it make whether we rescue others or not? What is the cause of our journey? It certainly includes our own rescue, our own discovery of who we are in Christ. However, it is much more than that.

Every day we are put to the test in our faith. Every day we find another obstacle from the enemy, a wall he tries to erect to keep us from ministering to those in need. Whether or not people realize we're in need of a Savior, many are being bound in the chains of abuse, neglect, depression, anxiety, addiction, sold into slavery, human trafficking, and much more. Even our very minds are being attacked by those who would promote their own agenda doing what's *"right in their own eyes"* (Isaiah 5:21).

The enemy (the devil) does not want you or anyone else to discover your true identity. If you do, you become an even bigger threat to him and his plan to destroy what God put into motion. The devil hates God. Because he cannot be part of God's magnificent plan and live in the beautiful eternity of heaven, he has been doing everything he can since the beginning to ruin eternity for God's people. Us.

Yet, the one thing we've studied over and over throughout this book is that he *is* defeated. He can't win... unless you allow him to. Remember, the only power the devil has is the power you give to him. Therefore, if you speak negatively either about others or yourself, you are giving the devil a foothold into their and your destruction.

Therefore, how do we prevent ourselves and others from sinking back into old habits, abuse and addictions?

> *It was for freedom that Christ set us free; therefore keep standing firm and do not be subject again to a yoke of slavery.*
> ~Galatians 5:1, NASB

If we stand firm in our faith in Jesus, we prevent ourselves from becoming slaves again to those old things that once held us down and prevented us from living in the freedom Christ died to give us.

It's a journey. It's a battle. It's a process. However, it's not too difficult; if it was, we wouldn't be able to do it. With Christ's help, of course, we can.

Be aware though, you will encounter people who will proclaim that it's just too hard to do. They have been tricked into believing that they can never get well, can never overcome illness, never get out of that abusive relationship, never get over addiction, depression, etc. They have been conditioned to believe they are nothing and mean nothing. These are the ones who are being lied to quite often by the very people they love the most. I understand. I have been there.

Still, we have a job to do, a mission. We are called to a great ministry, dear Warriors. But don't just take my word for it, take the word of the Apostle Paul:

I, therefore, the prisoner of the Lord, beseech you to walk worthy of the calling with which you were called, with all lowliness and gentleness, with longsuffering, bearing with one another in love, endeavoring to keep the unity of the Spirit in the bond of peace. ~Ephesians 4:1-3, NKJV

You and I are much more than we know. We can do this. It's not too difficult because we have Jesus on our side, walking with us through every minute of every day of our lives, even in the midst of trials. We can be brave. God has given us such great gifts to use in our journey.

You and I are much more than we know.

...in Christ Jesus our Lord,
in whom we have boldness and access with confidence
through faith in Him. ~Ephesians 3:11b-12, NKJV

God not only gave us Jesus as our Lord, but He also gave us a few other things through Him; boldness, confidence, faith, and access to the Father.

Not only are these things gifts, but they are also links to our identity. You, dear Mighty Warriors, are **bold**, **confident**, have **faith** and **have access to the Father**.

It's not just about living brave, living free, and having the confidence in Christ to walk our walk and walk in our anointing. We can run in our calling with freedom knowing that nothing, not even the devil, can stand in our way.

Knowing who we are in Christ, knowing who He says we are, we are free to worship and serve Him in ways that are deeper, more meaningful, and more abundant than we ever imagined possible. It's so exciting to live in such freedom from those chains that held us captive for so long. How much more exciting to be able to help others realize it, too!

If you look at Ephesians 3:14-21 (I used the New King James Version), you will find some amazing things.

The apostle Paul, writing to the church in Ephesus to encourage them, has given them a glimpse into the total love of God. It's sometimes difficult to fathom, even now. However, Paul gives us more than just a glimpse, and we can also find more links to our identity.

In verse sixteen we can see how Paul wished that God would grant us strength through His Spirit (the Holy Spirit), that Christ would dwell in our hearts through faith. But reading on, we find some links.

...that Christ may dwell in your hearts through faith; that you, being rooted and grounded in love,

May be able to comprehend with all the saints what is the width and length and depth and height –

To know the love of Christ which passes knowledge; that you may be filled with all the fullness of God.

~Ephesians 3:17-19, NKJV

Here, we find four more links to our identity in Christ. How awesome to discover we are ***rooted*** and ***grounded in love***, we have ***comprehension***, and we are ***filled with the fullness of God***. Maybe you wrote more than that, which is just fine. I hope the Holy Spirit spoke to you and showed you something else to your identity that only He wanted you to know. If so, how exciting! If we look past the verses above, we find one more link. Look below.

Now to Him who is able to do exceedingly abundantly above all that we ask or think, according to the power that works in us... ~Ephesians 3:20

In verse twenty you will find one more link to your identity. Through Christ, we have ***power***. His power works *in* us. It works *through* us. It is not our own, but His. However, it is part of who we are.

Ephesians 3:20-21 is also a doxology—a prayer of praise to God. We should praise Him every day, several times a day. He never tires of hearing us praise Him. We should never tire of praising Him. Because, without Him, where would we be? Certainly not here, discovering who we are in Him.

God has chosen us to be Christ's representatives on earth.

What a marvelous position. How humbling to know He loves us, chose us, saves us, heals us, promotes us, and sends us. It's overwhelming to know this much alone, but to consider the magnitude of our calling and what that means is priceless.

Dear, Mighty Warriors, have you realized who you are? Do you know how far you've come in this journey? Why then, would you even consider going back into your old ways? Why would you pick back up old habits? Why would you ever think you could wear those broken chains again? You can't.

It would be a great disservice to the LORD, our covenant maker and keeper, to retreat. Therefore stand, dear friends! Stand in your newly found identity. Raise your chin just a little higher, smile that beautiful smile, raise your hands in victory and praise to the One who has saved us, healed us, and made a way for us to be more than victorious.

Hallelujah! He is worthy!

Freedom. Bravery. These are two words which may seem foreign to you, but as you begin your new journey in who you are in Christ, you will begin to realize how powerful they are and how important to your journey.

It is time for us as God's Mighty Warriors to stand not only in our identity, but our calling. It is time to rise up and take our place in history, for we were not placed here by accident. Oh, no, friends, we are right where we are on purpose *for such a time as this.*

This is our time. While the world rages and others march for one thing or another, we know the truth, God's truth, Jesus. We know what we are to do. It's time to stand and do it.

Don't be afraid.

Be free.

Be brave.

Debriefing:

In this chapter we have discussed the importance of living not only free but brave. We have talked about what it means to be slaves to the things that keep us in bondage; however, we have also talked about what it means to be a slave of Christ. Jesus freed us, so it is very important for us to stay free, live free, and live brave so we can minister to others who are in bondage and help them discover their freedom and who they are in Christ. We are Christ's representatives here on earth, chosen to bring a most loving word to those seeking freedom.

Be sure to write all the links you found to your identity on your **Who I Am in Christ** *page.*

Further Reading:
Galatians 4
Ephesians 3 - 4

Who I Am in Christ

This is where I want you to write all those links to your identity in Christ. Write them close together so you'll have enough room. Fill this page. You will be glad you did when we finish this book.

What Do All Those Links Mean?

We have been writing words through this entire book. We have called them links to our identity. But what do all those links mean? Although they each describe who we are in Christ, as I was writing my earlier book for women, *Warrior Princess*, I discovered something powerful. Have you discovered it?

Look back at the Who I Am In Christ page. If you only look at the words, you'll definitely see a plethora of descriptive words, which alone tell an amazing story about the awesome person who wrote them down. You. I hope your inner warrior has been awakened and the fires ignited afresh. As we stand together, Mighty Warriors, I want to show you one more piece of armor that you may not have noticed was being weaved, link by link, throughout this study.

As we have written down each descriptive word, each link has been forming what is known as chainmail. What is chainmail? In medieval times, chainmail, or mail as it was often called, was tiny links of metal which was forged, then woven, or linked, together to form one large piece. It was then sewn onto a shirt as a protection against the blows of a sword, arrow, or other weapon used by the enemy. Think of it as a bullet-proof vest of today. Chainmail was also used to make hoods worn in helmets to protect the head and neck, as well as on the arms and legs, hands, and even the feet, all under metal armor, all used for protection. Of course, with any armor, it did not protect completely against an attack, but it did lessen the blow when struck.

Now, in regards to the links you wrote on Who I Am In Christ, let's do one more activity. Go back through each word, each link written, and circle each word. Let your circles overlap. Notice how the chainmail begins to form. When you embrace those words, those links to your identity, each link begins to intertwine. Just as chainmail becomes stronger when linked together, so do your links, Mighty Warrior! The next time the enemy comes prowling, scheming, plotting and whispering lies, trying to attack you, discourage you, or make you back down from your God-given calling, you remember that you have your chainmail on under your full armor of God. Straighten your crown, dear Mighty Warrior! Remember who you are and Whose you are. Put your foot on the neck of your enemy, the devil.* Then raise your Sword (your Word of God) and strike true.

You are victorious, O Mighty Warrior!

*To put your foot on the neck of your enemy is a show of authority. In Joshua 10, the LORD had given Joshua and the people of Israel the victory over five evil kings and their people and land. The word is, "Don't ever be afraid or discouraged," and "Be strong and courageous." The same applies to us today! Put your foot on the neck of your enemy, the devil, for Jesus has given you victory!

Further Reading:
Joshua 10:16-27
Luke 10:18-20

Debriefing

It is your business to restore the integrity and the righteousness in the high places of this land, and let the people see examples which will be helpful to them in their Christian life.

~Henry Drummond, *A Life for a Life and Other Addresses* (1893)

Discovering your identity in Christ is a lifelong journey. The links in this study are only the beginning. God's Word says so much more about you and to you if you'll but take the time to search.

With those links, those descriptive words, comes a calling so profound and magnificent it can bring us to our knees in humility. Like Moses, who are we that God would choose us to bring His Word to others? Yet, He has. He has bestowed such a gift upon us; how can we refuse?

There is an army rising up. This is an army of men and women, chosen by the Most High God. This army has God's favor. They are each called into various areas to bring good news. That good news is you don't have to live in captivity any longer. There is a way out. Jesus provided the way. All you have to do is step into it. He will do the rest.

God is raising up an army of men and women throughout the world. However, we must know who we are in Him before we can stampede into the masses and be successful. When we figure out who we are then we step into our identity and role as Mighty Warrior.

We are royal.

We are more than conquerors.

We are His.

Men and women have been oppressed for far too long. It is time for God's Mighty Warriors to arise and take their place as not only watchmen, but rescuers. There are many Warriors (watchmen, rescuers, preachers, teachers, etc.) out there already, working, serving, ministering. But they need help.

Once you know who you are in Christ, you become more powerful. You become more aware. You become who God specifically designed you to be. You also become an even bigger threat to the enemy. So, wear your armor at all times. Be prepared. Yet, also be brave.

The battle is not ours, but the Lord's. He will fight for us, with us, and through us, if we will be obedient and stand in faith for Him. We may need to stand still to win the battle. We may need to run at the enemy to win the battle. Though, make no mistake, we *will* win. The fight is fixed. We will be victorious, but we must make a move. Idleness will win us nothing.

Being a Mighty Warrior is more than just about being a warrior. It's about standing up for you—it's about being who you are in Him in such a way that it draws others to you. That's how you rescue your brothers and sisters in Christ.

Others will see each of us and be drawn to Christ in us. The Holy Spirit draws people to each of us. When we walk in our anointing, operate in our calling, boldly, with confidence, knowing who we are in Christ will emit a wonderful fragrance that some people cannot resist. That's when the door is open for you to minister.

Being a Mighty Warrior is so much more than just discovering who we are in Christ. We must walk it out every day. We must exercise the gifts He has given us. We must be alert every day to recognize when He has placed someone in our path to encourage, inspire, and rescue.

Some may not know what it is, but they know there's something different about you. You, friends, are called to bring healing and hope to your brothers and sisters so they can realize they are a Mighty Warrior, too.

Please note, this is not a competition. It's not a comparison. We each are unique and we should operate in our uniqueness. It would be pretty dull if we were all the same and had the same gifts. Yet the LORD uses many of the same gifts in us, just in different ways, which adds volumes to our uniqueness...still, we serve the same Lord. He never changes, although the more we serve Him the more He changes us. How exciting this is!

Jesus gives us the freedom to choose our walk. He gives us freedom to live abundantly our life journey here on earth and one day we will transition into eternity where we will continue to live abundantly forever. How awesome to think while we were here on earth, we helped Him to rescue others to live out that abundance.

Wouldn't it be exciting to know someday in eternity that we were the vessel He used to cause a domino effect of people helping rescue people out of the clutches of the enemy? I think so. Until then, we have a wonderfully magnificent calling.

You are a Mighty Warrior!

Stand tall, stand strong, keep your armor on and encourage those around you. If I never meet you in person here, I will meet you in eternity and we will celebrate.

Yours in God's Army,

Shelley

What Does a Mighty Warrior Look Like?

Maybe you're wondering what a Mighty Warrior actually looks like. He looks like you! In the Kingdom of God, we are all the same while also different. In the picture(s) below this, my dear Warriors, is an army rising up. They are fathers, sons, brothers, grandfathers, encouragers, prayer warriors, supporters, worshipers, and so much more. But most importantly, they are Sons of the Most High God! Come on in. They have scooched over so you can plant yourself in the midst of the group, for you, too, are a Mighty Warrior! So, place your own picture right there in the midst of them and join the ranks!

Many thanks to the Warriors who gave their time to support this project. You mean the world to me. I love each and every one of you dearly.

Appendix A:
How to Accept Jesus

There have been many "How To's" written on how to be saved; how to ask Jesus into your heart for salvation and eternal life. It can get confusing. I was once there myself and allowed the process to become so difficult I spent years wondering if I had "done it right."

If you are not sure whether you will go to heaven when you die, if you're not sure you know Jesus as your Lord and Savior, please allow me to introduce you to Him. He's a wonderful Friend.

There are a few things you need to know:

Everyone messes up. We all sin. Even Christians. But Jesus made a way for us to get to Heaven, and it's easier than people believe it is.

First, know that you've sinned and cannot get to heaven on your own merit.

Second, acknowledge that Jesus died for you, but rose from the dead just like He said He would.

Third, ask Him to forgive you of your sins and ask Him to come into your heart and be your Lord and Savior.

That's it!

Maybe you aren't sure exactly how to do that. Below is a step-by-step way to accept Jesus. Really, there's no right or wrong way to do it as long as you are sincere and humble when you address Jesus. But know this: He is so very loving, patient, and kind. He knows your heart and when you come to Him humbly, simply asking that He forgive you and save you, HE DOES! He promises that.

Now it's your turn. Below is a prayer that you can recite to receive salvation. Just remember to be sincere and humble. And believe in your heart.

"Jesus, I know I have sinned and messed up. But Your Word says that all who call upon You shall be saved. I'm sorry for the things I've done and ask Your forgiveness. Please save me and come into my heart. Thank You, Lord, for eternal life. In Jesus' name. Amen."

If you sincerely prayed that prayer, then Jesus promises that you are now saved. Your name is written in the Book of Life. You are on your way to heaven. That's it! Welcome to the Family of God!

Now, go tell someone!

Endnotes

Note from the Author

Reference to Beth Moore Bible study taken from *Stepping UP, a journey through the Psalms of Ascent,* ©2007 Beth Moore, Published by LifeWay Press

Valley of Dry Bones

Ezekiel 37:4b, 14b, New Living Translation
Ezekiel 37:1-14, New Living Translation
John 20:21, New Living Translation
John 20:22, New Living Translation
Ezekiel 37:11, New Living Translation
Ezekiel 37:14, New Living Translation
John 10:10, Amplified Bible
Hebrews 4:14-15, New Living Translation
Hebrews 4:12-13, New Living Translation
Psalm 33:13-15, New Living Translation
Psalm 32:7-8, New Living Translation
Further Reading:
Ezekiel 37:1-20
Psalm 32

Battle Lines

Quote from Bernard Law Montgomery, *Brainy Quotes,*
https://www.brainyquote.com/quotes/keywords/battle.html
Genesis 3:1, Amplified Bible
1 Corinthians 14:33, New King James Version
2 Timothy 1:7, New King James Version
James 4:7-8, Amplified Bible

James 4:10, New Living Translation
Ephesians 6:17, New Living Translation
2 Corinthians 10:3, New King James Version
2 Corinthians 10:4-6, New King James Version
1 Peter 5:8-9, Amplified Bible
1 Peter 5:7
Psalm 55:2-3
2 Corinthians 10:3, New Living Translation
2 Corinthians 10:7-8, New Living Translation
Luke 10:18-20, New King James Version
Further Reading:
Isaiah 14:12-23
James 4:7
2 Corinthians 10:3-6

Basic Training
Quote from Donna Partow, *The Complete Guide to Christian Quotations*, © 2011 by Barbour Publishing, Inc.
Romans 12:2, Amplified Bible
Psalm 119:11, New Living Translation
Matthew 4:1-11, New King James Version
2 Corinthians 1:3-7, New Living Translation
Hebrews 4:14-15, New Living Translation
Genesis 2:18, New Living Translation
Jeremiah 1:5, Amplified Bible
Ephesians 1:4, New Living Translation
1 John 4:1-6, The Message
Acts 17:28-29, New Living Translation
Further Reading:
Psalm 119:11
Matthew 4:1-11

Your Assignment

Quote from Rich Mendola, *The Complete Guide to Christian Quotations,* © 2011 by Barbour Publishing, Inc.

Ezekiel 33:7-9, New Living Translation

Jeremiah 1:5-12, New Living Translation

Romans 11:29, New Living Translation

Isaiah 55:11, New King James Version

Mark 6:4, New Living Translation

Esther 3:8-13, 4:1-14, New Living Translation

Judges 4:4-24, New King James Version

Psalm 91:14, New Living Translation

1 John 5:4-5, New Living Translation

Romans 8:37, New Living Translation

Romans 8:17, New Living Translation

Further Reading:

Esther 8-9

Jeremiah 1:5-12

Judges 4:4-24

Prepare for Battle

Quote from Stormie Omartian, www.topfamousquotes.com

Ephesians 6:10-11, New Living Translation

Ephesians 6:12, New Living Translation

Ephesians 6:13, New Living Translation

Ephesians 6:14-17, New Living Translation

1 Corinthians 14:33, English Standard Version

John 8:41-44, New King James Version

Matthew 7:7-8, New Living Translation

Ephesians 6:18, New Living Translation

Exodus 14:13-14, Expanded Bible

Further Reading: Ephesians 6:10-20

Worship is Warfare
Part One: Stand
Quote from Rick Renner, *The Complete Guide to Christian Quotations*, © 2011 by Barbour Publishing, Inc.
Deuteronomy 31:8, New Living Translation
2 Chronicles 20:1-23, New Living Translation
Matthew 6:33, New Century Version
2 Chronicles 20:19, New Living Translation
2 Chronicles 20:24-25, New Living Translation

Part Two: There's a Time to Run
1 Samuel 17:1-3, New Living Translation
1 Samuel 17:8-10, New Living Translation
James 4:7-8a, New Living Translation
James 4:26, New Living Translation
Deuteronomy 14:2, New King James Version
Deuteronomy 28:13, New King James Version
1 Samuel 17:47b, New Living Translation
Further Reading:
2 Chronicles 20:1-30
1 Samuel 16-17

Arise, O Mighty Warrior!
Quote from David Wilkerson, *The Complete Guide to Christian Quotations,* © 2011 by Barbour Publishing, Inc.
Judges 6:11-12, The Message
Judges 6:13, The Message
Judges 6:14, The Message
Judges 6:15-16, New King James Version
Judges 6:17-22, The Message
Judges 6:23, The Message

Psalm 118:17, New King James Version
Judges 6:24-32, New King James Version
Judges 6:33-35, New King James Version
Judges 7:2, New King James Version
Isaiah 51:4-8, The Message
Isaiah 51:12-23, New King James Version
Isaiah 51:16, New King James Version
Isaiah 51:21-23, New King James Version
Isaiah 52:3, New King James Version
Isaiah 52:7, New King James Version
Isaiah 52:12, New King James Version
Further Reading:
Isaiah 51:12-23
Isaiah 52:7-10

Live Brave, Live Free
Quote from Mel Lawrenz, *The Complete Guide to Christian Quotations,* © 2011 by Barbour Publishing, Inc.
John 8:36, New Living Translation
John 8:32, Berean Study Bible
1 Corinthians 7:22, New Living Translation
Definition of slave, www.dictionary.com
1 Peter 2:6, English Standard Version
2 Corinthians2:14-17, New Living Translation
Colossians 3:24, New Living Translation
Isaiah 5:21, New Living Translation
Galatians 5:1, New American Standard Bible
Ephesians 4:1-3, New King James Version
Ephesians 3:11b-12, New King James Version
Ephesians 3:14-21, New King James Version
Ephesians 3:17-19, New King James Version

Ephesians 3:20, New King James Version
Further Reading
Galatians 5
Ephesians 3 - 4

What Do All Those Links Mean?
Further Reading
Joshua 10:16-27
Luke 10:18-20

Debriefing
Quote from Henry Drummond, *The Complete Guide to Christian Quotations*, ©2011 by Barbour Publishing, Inc.

Other Titles by Shelley Wilburn

Walking Healed, A Journey of Forgiveness, Grace, and Hope

Written in diary form, Shelley Wilburn's book *Walking Healed* is her journey after being healed of over forty years of mental and emotional issues including depression, anxiety, and intimidation. Using snippets of her healing journey along with biblical truths, Shelley takes the reader on a journey of healing, forgiveness, grace, hope, and then leads into finding your purpose.

Written for those who suffer the pain and loneliness of depression and intimidation, Shelley reaches down in the black hole, finds those who are hurting, and helps them find their way out.

Walking Healed will help the reader realize that even Christians suffer depression. Shelley Wilburn knows and understands this from her personal experience. She also knows the freedom from these issues when God heals you and takes you on a wonderful journey of walking healed. Shelley's story of healing helps others know that even depression is curable and "nothing is impossible with God."

Walking Healed Companion Bible Study

As a companion to *Walking Healed*, the *Walking Healed Companion Bible Study* is a five-week journey into discovering healing, forgiveness, grace, hope, and finding your purpose. Designed to be used in conjunction with the *Walking Healed* book, Shelley Wilburn leads you into the depths of the Bible to discover healing for whatever holds you captive. She will then lead you in discovering forgiveness, God's grace, and the hope He gives us. In the final week, you will begin to discover how all these attributes converge to help you journey to discover your purpose in life.

Walking Healed and its companion study is designed to help women (and men) break free and live the life God intended for them. A definite must read. Available wherever books are sold.

Warrior Princess: Ignite Your Inner Warrior

One of the foundational principles in life is to understand who we are and what our purpose is in this life. But often, we find ourselves floundering.

Warrior Princess is a powerful, call-to-action Bible study for women, with journal and coloring pages tucked within the eight-week plan, that takes you on an interactive journey to discover your identity according to God's Word. Designed to awaken the inner warrior within the depths of your soul *Warrior Princess* will help you discover that you were chosen, and planned for, even before the foundations of the world, and what it truly means to be a daughter of the Most High God.

The Healing Path, A 30-Day Guide to Walking Healed and Living in Freedom

The Healing Path, a thirty-day devotional, is full of encouraging stories. Shelley Wilburn enlists the help of a few close friends as they take you on a deep dive into God's Word to illuminate the path before you. Inside, you will discover how to find healing and freedom from the obstacles that keep you from living in an abundant and enjoyable life. At the end of each day's devotion, you will also find further readings, Lights for Your Path, to illuminate your way to help keep you on the right path continuing your journey of walking healed and living in freedom.

About the Author

Shelley Wilburn is no novice when it comes to writing. She has been writing since she was twelve years old. She has authored several books, including the Walking Healed series, written for newspapers and women's magazines, written several articles and newsletters, and co-authored devotionals; as well as being a ghost writer, and doing freelance editing for others. In addition to writing, Shelley is also an avid reader, book reviewer, blogger, and speaker. She is the founder and president of Walking Healed Ministries which helps people who struggle with depression and anxiety find healing and wholeness through Jesus Christ. Shelley lives in southern Illinois with her husband, Don, and their two hilarious Chihuahuas, Georgie and Tootsie.

Shelley loves to hear from her readers.

You can find Shelley at:
Her website: www.shelleywilburn.org
Facebook: www.facebook.com/authorshelleywilburn
Instagram: www.instagram.com/shelleywilburn
Email her at shelley@shelleywilburn.org

CPSIA information can be obtained
at www.ICGtesting.com
Printed in the USA
LVHW010014130422
715558LV00002B/8